RIDGES and VAI

More Walks in the Midlands

by
Trevor Antill

Meridian Books

Published 1993 by Meridian Books.
© Trevor Antill 1993
ISBN 1-869922-20-4

Publishers' Note:

Every care has been taken in the preparation of this book and all the information has been carefully checked and is believed to be correct at the time of publication. However, neither the author nor the publishers can accept responsibility for any errors or omissions or for any loss, damage, injury or inconvenience resulting from the use of the book.

Please remember that the countryside is continually changing; hedges and fences may be removed or re-sited; landmarks may disappear; footpaths may be re-routed or be ploughed over and not reinstated (as the law requires); concessionary paths may be closed.

The publishers would be very pleased to have details of any significant changes that are observed by readers.

Meridian Books
40 Hadzor Road
Oldbury
Warley
West Midlands
B68 9LA

Printed in Great Britain by BPCC Wheatons Ltd., Exeter.

Contents

Also by the author:

Ridges and Valleys: Walks in the Midlands
The Navigation Way: A hundred mile towpath walk (second
edition) (*with Peter Groves*)

Introduction

In this, a second book of selected walks in the three counties of Shropshire, Staffordshire and Worcestershire, I have described eighteen new walks that follow the established theme of Ridges and Valleys. Some of the areas explored are among the lesser known parts of these historic counties while at the same time most of the walks contain some element of historic or local interest: for these reasons I believe this book offers the reader a real sense of discovery.

On a practical note readers should be prepared for the occasional slight difference between the descriptive text and what actually appears 'on the ground'. Whenever I walk a route and find anything untoward I report the matter to the relevant County Council. This can result in me describing, for example, 'cross a broken stile'. While the stile is broken — and probably still broken when I do the revision some six months later — the County Council may well have replaced it by the time the book is published.

In some of the text compass bearings are given. This does not mean that the walk is across difficult or featureless terrain however. On the contrary, in nearly all cases compass bearings are not required and directions such as '...go half left to the gate in the opposite hedge...' are more than adequate. However, the last few decades have seen the advent of huge 'prairie' type fields that have resulted from modern farming techniques where hedgerows have been grubbed out. In this circumstance a compass bearing can be a useful addition, as it also can during poor visibility. In such cases the bearing given is always quoted as Grid North rather than Magnetic North.

Finally, all the Rights of Way described in this book have been checked against the Definitive Maps held by the relevant County Councils. Likewise, all the walks have been independently checked by my 'squadron' of test pilots; Rex Evans, John Greatbatch, Peter Groves, Albert Purcell and Arthur Welch; to all of whom I am most grateful.

If you enjoy the walks as much as I have enjoyed planning, walking, revising and checking then you are surely in for a treat. All that remains now is to go out there; take in the views; keep fit; keep healthy; and to do so — keep walking!

Trevor Antill

'Age is but a measure of time — and time is a four letter word!'(TJA)

Location Map

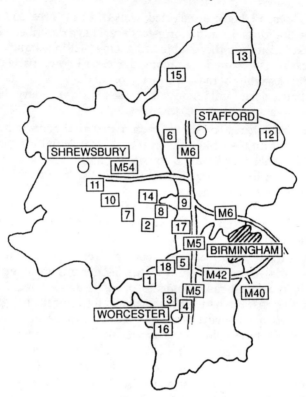

Transport

All the walks in this book are circular and should present no problems of access to motorists. Also, with one exception, they can be reached by public transport, although in a few cases this involves some extra walking – and some bus services in the more remote areas are somewhat sparse. Details are given in the introductory boxes to each walk. Because of the variability of services you should always check on times and routes before setting out. Some useful telephone numbers are:

British Rail (Birmingham): 021-643 2711

Bus Services: Hereford and Worcester, 0905-766800;
                Shropshire, 0345-056785;
                Staffordshire, 0785-223344
                West Midlands, 021-200 2700.

Walk 1
Beautiful Bewdley
Bewdley

This short walk is an ideal opportunity to view Bewdley – a unique Georgian riverside town – not only at close quarters but also with a panoramic aspect. Indeed the return leg gives majestic views across the Severn Valley and enables you to appreciate the town's past importance as a road and river trading centre. By following the walk with a tour of Bewdley and a visit to its imaginative town museum, you will fully appreciate the origin of its name – from the Norman French 'beautiful, fine place'. Bewdley is also an important station on the Severn Valley Railway.

DISTANCE: 3½ miles
MAPS: Landranger (1:50,000) 138
Pathfinder (1:25,000) 952
PARKING: Public car parks in Bewdley
PUBLIC TRANSPORT: Midland Red West Service 192/292 Birmingham - Hereford. Alight at Bewdley
START/FINISH: River bridge in Bewdley (GR 787754)

CROSS Telford's road bridge over the River Severn to the east bank and straight away go left towards Bridge House. Immediately passing the entrances to 'Woodeave' and 'Glenhurst' on the right you will arrive at the entrance to the Bowling Club, all in the matter of a few yards. Following the edge of the bowling green is a fenced footpath that you take to arrive at trees on the edge of a static caravan site. Here the footpath splits, the main one going ahead across the caravan site and the secondary one – yours – going right to follow the edge of the site with a holly hedge and wall on your right and caravans to your left. Soon this path takes you up to steps onto a narrow lane.

Directly opposite are more steps up to a footpath sign and a metal wicket gate onto the Severn Valley Railway line. Carefully cross the line to follow the obvious fenced path opposite as it rises up a bank and at the top bears right behind houses to meet another minor lane. Turn left along the lane and follow it for a third of a mile to the T-junction with Crundalls Lane immediately in front of Grey Green Farm.

Go left along Crundalls Lane and then soon right along the lane signed for 'Lightmarsh Farm Only'. In a short way the lane makes a sharp right turn but you continue forward to take the stile at the side of the gate on the corner. In the field continue on the same line to a stile in the hedge ahead, keeping a hillock on your left.

This hillock, with what appears to be a ditch and dyke at its base, gives me the distinct impression of being man made. I have made various enquiries and received varied opinions ranging from 'nothing of interest' to 'a deserted medieval village with a natural feature modified to make a Motte'. What is certain is that no one really knows and are not likely to until an archaeological excavation has been carried out. The site has been reported to the Archaeology Department at Hereford and Worcester County Council who have given it the Sites and Monuments Record Number 3994. At the time of writing I was unable to discover more, though I still feel it is too symmetrical in shape to be natural. What do you think?

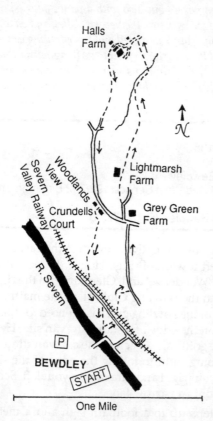

Crossing this second stile continue to a third, left of a bungalow, giving access onto the farm road to Lightmarsh Farm. On the road go left and, ignoring a stile in the right hand fence near the bungalow, walk up to the waymarked gate on the right of the farm and its buildings. Pass through it and immediately through a second to now follow the broad hedged and fenced track – ignoring another stile in the fence right – to a third gate. Through this one continue with the track, now with just a hedge and fence on your left, up to another gate and stile.

On the other side of this fourth gate follow the same line, with now a fence on your left, to a gate in the hedge in front that is a slightly off set field corner. Do not go through this gate but bear slightly right to follow

The man-made knoll?

the hedge and continue up in the same direction and parallel to the overhead power lines to your right.

In the top corner of this field there is a stile that you cross. In the next field you follow the same direction – still parallel to the power lines – to cut the field corner and then meet the trees on the field edge above a deeply gullied stream. The path now follows the field edge and gully to enter another field through a gap. On the same line your path now goes under the overhead cables and then passes a telegraph pole on the edge of the gully.

About 35 yards beyond the telegraph pole, and before the end of the field, go left down into the gully to cross a stile and plank footbridge. On the other side cross up the centre of the sloping field to gradually merge towards the third telegraph pole ahead where there is a stile in the fence. Cross the stile into a small field and continue forward with a garden hedge on your left to a gate and stile in the corner. This gives access onto a farm track.

At the track turn left and follow it – on the right is 'Greenacres' bungalow. Immediately past the bungalow the track splits. You take the secondary, right hand one to pass between a silo on the left and an orchard on the right. This secondary track is a little higher than the one you have just left and in front of Hall's Farm it swings right and then instantly left to take you between a metal barn on the right and a brick barn on the left. In front of you is a gate that you pass through into a field to follow a vehicle track forward. Just before the next gate ahead; which bears the legend 'Private Property – Keep Out'; bear left to a gate in the corner that has a stile partially camouflaged by the hedge.

Pass through the gate, or over the stile, to join a well defined broad track that follows the edge of the field with a hedge on your left. Ahead of you and to your right the views now open out across the Severn Valley to the Wyre Forest. Now follow the track down along the field edge to a gate in the bottom corner. Through the gate your track becomes hedged on both sides as you follow it to pass houses and soon merge into a tarmac lane at 'The Riddings'.

Continue with the lane for a third of a mile as it gradually descends and then arrives at riding stables. Go forward to pass the stables, with their large 'No Smoking' sign, and then reach the yellow painted 'Wood-land View'. Immediately past 'Woodland View' turn right into the service drive signed 'Crundalls Court' and go over the cattle grid. In a few yards the service drive swings left but you continue forward to leave the drive on the bend where there is a double step stile and a public footpath sign.

Cross over the stile into a field and follow the left hand wooden ranch fencing to its protruding corner. Leave the fence to go forward and cut the field corner to a stile next to a gate in the opposite hedge. Over this stile turn instantly right and follow the hedge down to another gate and stile. This takes you forward on the same line but now with a fence on your left and the hedge still on your right.

Soon entering another field through a gateway pause here to look across the roofs of Bewdley. Now bearing slightly left follow a well trodden path to the head of a small valley. Descend through the lowest part of the valley to a stile and bridge that takes you under the Severn Valley Railway and onto a narrow lane.

A left turn along the lane will take you past houses and Riverway Drive after which you will come to the main entrance to the static caravan site you met earlier. Pass through the gate and, where the gravel service road splits, go straight ahead over the grassy centre and then continue on to meet the path you followed past the bowling green at the start of your walk.

Now retrace your steps into Bewdley which, even on a Sunday, has just about anything you might need to keep body and soul together.

Walk 2
A Scenic Gateway
Morville

*At the junction of the A458 and the B4368, Morville has always appeared to me
as the gateway to the Corvedale. Sitting at the base of Aston Hill it is a mellow
village with the aura of a well maintained environment. Morville Hall is of
Elizabethan origin and is a tenanted National Trust property – it may only be
visited by written appointment with the tenant.*

DISTANCE: 4½ or 6½ miles
MAPS: Landranger (1:50,000) 138
Pathfinder (1:25,000) 911
PARKING: Lay-by on A458 (GR 675938)
PUBLIC TRANSPORT: Midland Red West Service 436/437 Bridgnorth -
Shrewsbury. Alight at Morville
START/FINISH: Opposite Haughton Lane, Morville (GR 672939)

FROM the lay-by on the A458 walk in a north-westerly direction
towards Morville. On the left-hand side of the road – immediately
before the entrance to 'Ercal House' and just before Haughton Lane
– there is a gate into a field. Go through it to swing left and up a concrete
track that passes behind the vicarage garden. In a short distance it arrives
at the entrance to a water treatment plant. Here you leave the concrete
to go right, and down, with the perimeter fence to the Mor Brook.

At the bottom corner swing left to walk between the perimeter fence
and the brook. Leaving the perimeter fence ignore a footbridge on the
right and follow the same line just below the edge of the trees. At the end
of the trees follow the base of the slope soon to meet the brook-side again
at a gate. Beyond the gate walk just above the stream, now on a clear
path, to then leave the pasture and enter trees. On leaving the trees –
ahead is a cottage – turn right to descend to the hunter's gate at the side
of the lane bridge over Mor Brook.

On the tarmac turn right and, ignoring the left turn, continue ahead to
follow the sign for Meadowley and Upton Cressett along this narrow
and little used lane. Although it is fairly steep, in hot weather it is
wonderfully shaded by its canopy of trees. In a little over half a mile you
will come to Upper Meadowley Farm.

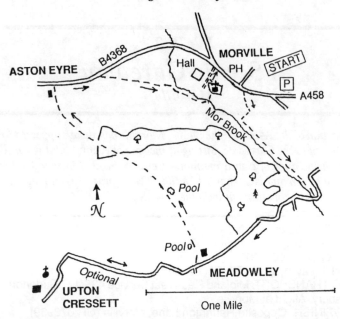

At this point, if time allows, you can make an interesting diversion to the redundant church at Upton Cressett. *Continue from* ➡ *below if you are going to omit this.* Simply continue along the lane to the church – and Upton Cressett Hall – where the lane promptly ends.

Upton Cressett is a fascinating place, steeped in history and still part of it. Upton (the Cressett came later) is an ancient Saxon settlement and in fields nearby are the remains (mounds) of a medieval village and a Roman dwelling. Though redundant, the church of St. Michael dates from early Norman times and has a long association with the families of 'de Upton' and 'Cressett' – hence the place name! Near the font are two bells; the larger dating from about 1300, the smaller from 1701. The oak porch is fourteenth century. Nearby Upton Cressett Hall is of Tudor origin.

To continue the walk retrace your steps to Upper Meadowley Farm where you turn left to the bridleway sign.

➡ If you decided not to make the diversion; then, at Upper Meadowley Farm, turn right to a bridleway sign.

Pass immediately left of old farm buildings – further left of you is a barn conversion – and then left of the gable ends of three modern barns. Here you will come to two gates. Go through the left one to enter the corner of a large field near a pool.

Walk ahead through the field heading for the far upper right corner – a bearing of 330 degrees. In this corner you will find a wooden hunter's gate. Go through it to follow a path between a hedge left and a pool right to arrive at a step stile into a field. In the field walk forward, with the hedge and fence to your left, on what is now a broad backed ridge with fine views to the Clees and Wenlock Edge. Just before the end of this field the left hedge gives way to a fence in which there is a stile. Ignore this stile and continue forward to a gate and stile near to a small stone and tile barn.

Ancient barn. Near Meadowley

In the next field continue in the same direction and begin a descent, initially following the left hedge and then gradually veering away from it into the bottom right corner. Here there is a gate with an old hunter's gate beside it while right is a new hunter's gate and next to that a waymarked step stile. Cross the stile onto a clear path that enters scrub. In a few yards this path diverges and the tendency is to draw you left. However take your time for in fact the true way briefly swings right, into the tree edge and out again, to then follow a fairly clear line left and down to a second waymarked stile into a field.

Though this path is fairly well walked and as a result is relatively free from overgrowth this situation could change if it were unused for any length of time, particularly in high summer. Should this happen, then, from the gate mentioned in the previous paragraph, follow the field edge forward and turn right down the adjacent field edge to pick up the line again at the second waymarked stile. This is only an alternative if the right of way is impassable.

Over this second stile continue forward across the slope – ahead is a good, elevated view of the lovely Aston Eyre – to a gate with a stile that you cross. Walk ahead on a slight embankment and immediately left of two trees to then descend gradually to a gate and stile in the far bottom corner. Now on a distinct fenced track proceed to a gate and two stiles where the track swings left. Leave the track by crossing the two stiles and maintaining your original direction along the edge of a field with the hedge on your right. Go through a gate to pass right of 'Lindown Cottage' and 'Apsley Cottage' and so reach the B4368.

Turn right along the road – passing a mile post – for about 400 yards to a gateway on the right that takes you into a large field where you are faced with a fairly long mid-field crossing. Ahead you will see the tower of Morville church for which you aim, slightly left and on a bearing of 100 degrees. Follow this line across the field until arriving at the bank of Mor Brook. Here go right with the fence, passing and ignoring a gate gap leading to a footbridge, to continue with the field edge to a point where it bears right, away from the brook, and where another field intervenes. In a further 65 yards, and opposite the church tower, you will come to a fence stile on your left over which you then walk the few yards to the gated bridge ahead.

Crossing the bridge now walk to the small gate in the hedge surrounding the church. Enter the churchyard and pass in front of the tower and then through the arch of the lych-gate. Now go left and through the gate at the side of a cattle grid and so walk to meet the drive of Morville Hall. Turn right and – accompanied on the left by the dry moat – pass through a kissing gate at the side of another cattle grid and then reach the A458. Turn right to pass 'The Acton Arms' and so return to the start.

Walk 3
A Timely Brew
Chaddesley Corbett

Chaddesley Corbett is one of those old country villages that are popular with retired people – very handy for a summer drive and a pub lunch! A picturesque backwater just off a main road it has many black and white timber framed buildings – some real, some imagined. More importantly it is the start of an attractive and easily followed walk.

Only a little over a mile away, and well worth a visit, is the historic Harvington Hall – famous for its many priest holes – whilst in Chaddesley Corbett 'The Talbot' and 'The Swan' have, between them, possibly the best two real ale brews in the Midlands.

DISTANCE: 5 miles
MAPS: Landranger (1:50,000) 139
Pathfinder (1:25,000) 953
PARKING: Roadside in Chaddesley Corbett
PUBLIC TRANSPORT: Midland Red West Services 133/134 (Kidderminster - Bromsgrove). Alight at Chaddesley Corbett Turn and walk north to St. Cassian's church
START/FINISH: St. Cassian's church (GR 892736)

TAKING the public footpath opposite St. Cassian's church, walk along the surfaced lane to a point opposite barns on the right. Follow the lane as it swings left and then right to pass a barn conversion. Continue with it for another 250 yds where it spills into a field. Entering the field follow the left-hand hedge to the far corner where you cross a stile adjacent to a small pool. Continuing forward across the next field and on the same line – the paths are well trodden in this area – cross another stile just before the power lines. In the next field go under the overhead lines and enter Chaddesley Wood over a stile.

Created in 1973 through the generosity of John Cadbury, Chaddesley Wood is now a national nature reserve consisting of 102 hectares. An outstanding example of lowland oakwood, Chaddesley and the neighbouring woods were originally part of the ancient Royal Forest of Feckenham and are thought to have descended from the first primaeval forest. Today the reserve is managed to provide a good mix of tree and shrub so that in turn it can support a diverse

Ridges and Valleys II

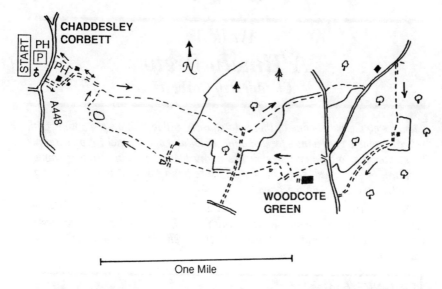

CHADDESLEY CORBETT

WOODCOTE GREEN

One Mile

collection of plant and animal species – the badger being particularly strong. Incorporated in the woodland is a waymarked 'Jubilee Walk' inaugurated in 1977 to mark the Queen's 25th anniversary of accession to the throne.

From the stile continue forward for some way along a distinct path through the trees, following the occasional yellow waymark arrows. At the top of a short incline you will come to a broad cross track with a waymark on a tree. Turn left and in only a few yards – where it bears left – leave the track to continue forward on a broad, distinct and gradually rising grassy path. Coming to the woodland edge you will see a stile – near a notice board – that you cross to leave the woods and enter a sloping field. On the same line as before and keeping the woodland on your left follow its edge to meet a narrow surfaced lane. Cross it and take the path directly opposite to then cross a stile back into woodland. The path is initially sunken but then follows the perimeter before bearing left to a stile at the side of a bungalow. Over the stile go forward with the drive to meet a road.

A left turn along the road will take you past 'Randan Cottage' on the left and then to a public bridleway on the right signed for 'Randan Wood'. Enter the well used bridleway and, ignoring a hunter's gate on the left, follow it to another hunter's gate through which the way now follows the woodland edge along a fenced track and past Highwood Cottage – this bridleway can be muddy!. Just beyond the cottage go right with the track, which is now an unsurfaced road, and then through a gate to continue forward around a right turn immediately before the road at Woodcote Green.

Right along the road will eventually bring you to a road junction on a bend. Immediately before it a telegraph pole on the left marks a stile into a field. Enter the field and walk ahead to the opposite corner where you cross a stile into a narrow enclosure. Ahead is a gate and stile that takes you forward onto a concrete farm road. Continue on the same line along the concrete and through a gate to then bear slightly right to another gate with a stile at the side, all the time keeping right of the farm. In only a few yards the concrete ends and you turn right to cross a bridged ditch into a sloping field.

Walk slightly left to a gate and fence set in the corner of a hedge. As you near it you will see the stile in the fence. Go over and turning left follow the fence taking care to walk between it and the pool surrounded by oak trees. This will bring you to a stile and so into another field where you continue forward, now with a hedge on your right, for its whole length. Eventually you will arrive in a corner where you then cross a stile and a plank footbridge to meet a cross track.

Chaddesley Corbett churchyard

Go left along the track for no more than 15 yards where on the right is another plank footbridge. Cross it and enter the fenced path that follows the edge of Chaddesley Wood. At the woodland corner cross a stile and follow the same line to arrive at another stile in a hedge. Entering a large field continue forward across the middle, under the overhead power lines, and aim for the oak to the right of a clump of trees.

Cross the track leading to Tagg Barn and continue forward passing close to the oak tree and so along the left edge of this next field. Over a brow a nice view appears across to Chaddesley Corbett and its church – your ultimate destination. Walk down to the field corner and crossing the stile walk to another left of the pool. Now walk between the hedge and the pool to a stiled gate in the corner.

From here, older maps show the right of way going straight ahead across the middle of the next field and heading for the church steeple. However it was diverted some years ago and the new way is now described.

In this next field turn immediately right to the corner and then left to

The footpath in Chaddesley Woods

a protruding corner. Here go right with the waymark arrow for 100 yards, keeping the hedge on your right, to reach a step stile in the hedge. Crossing over, continue your line but with the hedge now on your left. This will bring you to the hedged green lane of your outward journey where you turn left to reach the barn conversion. Instead of going left with the green lane here, go straight ahead over the fence stile next to the sign for the Chaddesley Corbett Parish Council Allotment Site. Walk forward with the direction of the waymark arrow following a line of wooden poles and keeping right of a low embankment. The path now takes you between houses and through a green metal gate to arrive at the main village street in front of 'The Swan'. Turn left to pass 'The Talbot' and so return to the parish church.

*Common White
Inocybe*

Walk 4
Peewit Patrol
Grimley

This walk follows part of the Severn Valley above Worcester and returns by way of a terrace rather than a ridge. Nonetheless it is a very attractive half day walk with several features of interest, not least being the aerial displays of courting lapwings at the appropriate season. Look out for flocks of Canada Geese and the occasional clump of riverside mistletoe.

Resting in Elgar country the walk starts from a lay-by on the A443 near the tiny riverside village of Grimley.

DISTANCE: 5 miles
MAPS: Landranger (1:50,000) 150
Pathfinder (1:25,000) 974 & 996
PARKING: Lay-by on A443
PUBLIC TRANSPORT: Midland Red Services 293/304 (Kidderminster - Worcester) to Grimley Lane (A443).
START/FINISH: Lay-by on A443 (GR 829604)

FROM the lay-by walk northwards along the A443 for approximately 200 yards where a minor road, signed for Grimley, goes off to the right. Turn right along it and in only a few yards you will see a red Post Office letter box on the left next to a wooden kissing gate. Go through the kissing gate and head straight across the field aiming for a point just slightly left of the church tower in the distance. This line will bring you to another kissing gate which you go through to continue in the same direction.

Arriving at a low embankment go up it to pass through the metal kissing gate in the fence corner. Now following the left hand fence arrive at power lines and a pole. Go forward to join the fence and wall surrounding the churchyard and follow it forward where in just a few yards you will see a wooden kissing gate in the wall. Go through and pass immediately right of the sandstone St. Bartholomew's church to then descend steps through a gateway into a lane opposite a bungalow.

Here turn left to pass the Wagon Wheel Inn and so swing right with the lane as it now becomes unsurfaced. Now follow the lane to its

termination at the riverside. Just
before the river bank there is a
footbridge and fence stile on the
right that you cross over to walk
south, downstream with the River
Severn. To your left and across the
river is the Hawford Ridge.

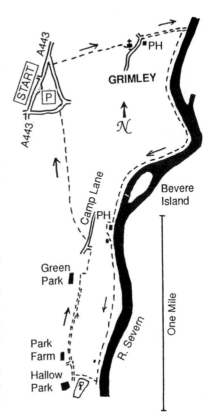

Staying with the river, in a while
you will come to Bevere Island –
so named after beavers who
visited it before becoming extinct
in this country – and soon its river
lock. Before the lock, cross a step
stile immediately in front of a
large navigation arrow pointing
right. Continue forward along the
well maintained lock side to pass
the lock-keeper's control 'tower'
to then follow the bank-side path
towards the remote, riverside
Camp House Inn where you can
often watch rowers sculling up
from Worcester.

*Here the Ordnance Survey map
shows the right of way continuing
between the inn and the river but
wash erosion has destroyed the path
making it necessary to take the following short diversion.*

Crossing the step stile next to the inn turn immediately right along the
fenced path that follows the side of the inn and arrives at its frontage.
Now turn left to pass a sign stating 'Please keep clear, entrance to back
car park' and with a fence on your left continue forward – soon leaving
the fence – to pass right of a white, and then a green, wooden chalet
where immediately before a brick house you swing left to a white gate.
Go through this gate to rejoin the riverside.

Continuing downstream with the riverside right of way, cross a series
of stiles until entering a field containing, in the corner, a rectangular
corrugated sheet structure topped with barbed wire. Here follow the
river to the end of this field where, immediately before another riverside
stile, you need to turn right and follow the left hand hedge and fence.

Above and forward of you are the seven (can you count more?) white chimneys of Hallow Park. Going through a gap in the hedge ahead, pass a gate on the left, and continue forward to a step stile in another hedge near the field corner. Cross over and walk up the bank to meet a crossing track.

Turning right along this crossing track follow it up to a gate and stile immediately before the barn conversions at Park Farm. Continue forward to pass right of the conversions to another gate. Now follow the grassy track as it begins its descent, through another gate, where at the bottom it meets another track coming in from the right. Directly ahead of you in the bottom corner is a gate and step stile. Cross the stile into a fenced track and follow it forward to a wooden gate and step stile.

To the right is a small stand of trees. To your left is the Graeco-Roman architecture of Green Park.

Continue forward, with the trees on your right, to another gate immediately right of two grand pedestal dove cotes. Cross the step stile at the side of the gate and turn right to follow the other edge of the trees to yet another gate.

Do not go through this gate, instead turn left to follow the field edge with the fence on your right. At the next field corner cross two stiles in quick succession to enter a fenced track. Here turn left to the green metal gates and cross the metal step stile to their right and so onto a cobbled drive/lane. To your left are the ornate gates of Green Park.

On the cobbles go right between a footpath and a bridleway sign. In about 30 yards you will come to a fence stile on the left. Cross the stile and follow the fenced path along the side of earthworks to a step stile into a field. In the field continue forward with the hedge and fence on your left to the opposite corner where you go left over a fence stile and immediately right over a step stile into the next field. On the same line follow the field edge, again with a fence and hedge on your left, to the next corner where you cross a step stile into a few trees. A few yards ahead is another step stile into a field. Cross this and follow the same direction as before again with the fence and hedge on your left. In the next corner a fence stile awaits you. Cross it and follow the left hand fence up to a step stile that gives access onto a minor road.

At the road cross over to the opposite pavement and turn right. Stay with the road as it swings left past a T-junction and follow the road sign for 'Great Witley 7' and 'Stourport 8'. In a while you will pass the red Post Office letter box that marked the beginning of your walk.

Walk 5
Relics Ancient And Modern
Halesowen

Constantly under the eye of the developer, the area of green belt between the M5 motorway and the Clent Hills is blessed with a multitude of public footpaths that are of critical importance as an escape for the urbanised population of the West Midlands. Easily accessible from any part of the Midlands, this walk uses some of those paths and also takes in three historic architectural features from widely differing eras. As such, it is a varied route that has something to interest most people.

DISTANCE: 7 miles
MAPS: Landranger (1:50,000) 139
Pathfinder (1:25,000) 933 & 953
PARKING: Roadside in Lye Close Lane on west side of motorway bridge (GR 988827). Lay-by on unclassified road near Illeybrook Farm (GR 974821)
PUBLIC TRANSPORT: WMT Services 9/19. Alight on Manor Way (A456) at the Black Horse (not the one that you will meet later at Illey). Walk west down the hill for about 50 yds to a stile and a footpath sign to Illey on the left. Cross the stile, go through the field and cross another stile. Aiming towards the ruins of St Mary's Abbey, which you can see ahead, cross a stream by a footbridge and turn left with a hedge on your right. Now pick up the main route at the point marked ➤ on page 23.
START/FINISH: Lye Close Lane (GR 988827)

IMMEDIATELY over the motorway bridge – on the west side – there is a T-junction. To the right is Lapal Lane South and to the left Lye Close Lane which is also signed as a public footpath and a 'No Through Road'. Go left (south) along Lye Close Lane and follow it as it descends and swings right to a point where the tarmac ends at two cottages and a gated stile.

Cross the stile, which is signed 'Public Footpath – Illey and Waseley', and continue forward on a hedged path down to a junction of paths. Here go left.

Pass under overhead power cables and then walk to the top of a slight

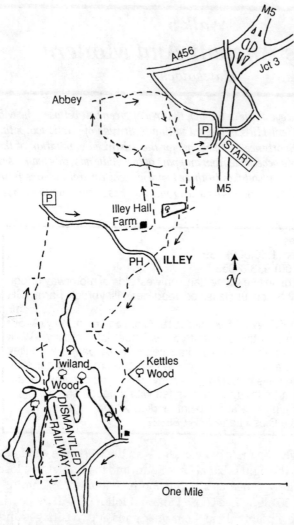

rise where there is a gate left and a gate and stile right. In front are upright wooden poles that act as vehicle barriers.

Do not cross the stile on the right but instead go forward through the barrier poles along a hedged path, eventually to reach trees and a stream beyond which is a step stile. Go over and turn instantly right to quickly meet a gate and stile. In the next field walk half left across the pasture to a stile in the hedge. Over this turn half right with the direction of the waymark arrows and walk to the bottom left corner and a stream. Go left with a track and the stream to soon cross the stream to a gate and stile into a hedged track. Now follow this track up, passing a stile on the right, to pass right of old farm buildings and through a kissing gate onto the road almost opposite the 'Black Horse' pub.

Cross over the road and turn left for the few yards necessary to reach the footpath sign on the right for Romsley and Waseley. Go right with the unsurfaced track as initially it follows the edge of the pub car park

The Black Horse, Illey

Photo: Pat Arrowsmith

and rises to a slight crest. Ahead and across the valley are views of the Clent Hills.

At the crest continue with the track as it descends to Illey House Farm where you will meet a three way path signpost. Staying with your track for Romsley descend and then rise to a stiled gate. On the other side pass left of a house and continue forward past outbuildings to another gate and stile. In the field swing half right down to a footbridge and over a stream.

On the other side ignore the line of waymarked posts to the right (the Illey Way) and instead swing left with a tractor track to join the left hand hedge. Following it to the field corner you will find a stile. In the next field go left diagonally across the field – a bearing of 115 degrees – to a gate and stile in the far hedge. Now go ahead and through the middle of the following field to aim for the protruding corner of Kettles Wood, a bearing of 165 degrees. Arriving there cross the plank footbridge and step stile.

Now you are at a junction of paths. One goes straight ahead along the edge of the wood, the other – yours – goes half right across the corner of the field on a bearing of 210 degrees to a white gate and step stile next to an oak tree.

Go over the stile and in this field go diagonally across – 180 degrees – towards a fence and trees above a gully. Arriving at the fence go left and follow it to the top of the field where there is a ladder stile in the corner. Over the ladder stile go forward to pass right of a house, garages and a shed with a 'No Smoking' sign. Here join a concrete drive and follow it to a road where you turn right.

The remains of Halesowen Abbey
Photo: Pat Arrowsmith

Now follow the road to pass the entrance to Newbrook Farm on the left and in another 100 yards go right to the recessed, white, double gates that have a kissing gate at the side. Go through and follow the hedged track forward to pass a derelict building and then meet a gate below a dismantled railway bridge. Crossing the fence stile at the side of the gate continue along the track down to the bottom of a small valley. As you will see, this valley becomes a substantial gorge further on.

At the valley bottom, and immediately before the stream, there is a junction of paths. Turn right – you are now back on the Illey Way – and follow the bottom edge of the long field with the stream on your left. Across the field and right you will see the tree covered embankment of the old Halesowen Railway. Your path and the embankment are now on a converging course and eventually meet past the end of the field. At this point there is a gap where you enter Twiland Wood to then follow the pleasant path to the remains of brickwork, just before a gateway.

In days gone by a substantial railway structure known as the Dowery Dell Viaduct crossed the gorge on your left. At 660 feet long, supported by two brick abutments and eight cast iron trestles, it towered a 100 feet above the stream in the valley bottom. Dismantled in 1965, the occasional overgrown abutment is the sole evidence of an outstanding feat of engineering.

Just through the gateway, steps descend steeply left down to the

The Infirmary, Halesowen Abbey
Photo: Pat Arrowsmith

bottom of the gorge. Crossing the culverted stream climb the opposite bank to emerge at the edge of a large field by a footpath signpost. This directs you forward and across the centre of the field on a well trodden path. Just over the brow of the field you will see a stile and another footpath signpost at a junction of paths in the fence ahead. Go over the stile and continue forward – thus now leaving the Illey Way – to the opposite field boundary where you cross a footbridge. On the other side follow the same line to pass left of an oak tree and reach a field corner where beneath another oak there is a fence stile.

In the next field go forward with the hedge on your right to another fence stile in the field corner. Go forward again in the next field to yet another stile in the fence ahead. This time cross the stile and go forward for 25 yards to the protruding right hand hedge corner. At this point there is a cross path – not very obvious on the ground – and a black and white 'public footpath' sign pointing right. While this is correct it is not the path that you need. Yours instead leaves the hedge to continue ahead across the field – a bearing of 355 degrees, nearly due north – to the protruding hedge corner almost opposite.

Arriving at the opposite corner there is a fence stile just a yard or two along. Cross over it and go forward on the same line and with the hedge on your right to the entrance of a green lane in the field corner. Here enter the mouth of the lane for a mere 10 feet where in the left hedge you will see a step stile under an oak tree. Go over it into another field where you turn immediately right to cross the sloping field heading for double wooden electricity poles that are left of dwellings. At the poles and behind them is a stile and a footbridge that you cross to walk between a fence and stream to another stile onto a road.

At the road turn right and stay with it for some way to pass the 30 mph signs and then, on the left, arrive at a public footpath sign for 'Manor Way via Abbey Ponds'. At this sign continue with the road for a further 75 yards to go left to the gate and stile on the drive to Illey Hall Farm.

Follow the drive to pass a stile left and then turn right with a sign and arrow on the brick wall of an outbuilding just before the farmhouse. This takes you through a gate into a field containing a football pitch and pavilion where you instantly turn left to follow the hedge to a corner and two stiles. Crossing the left hand one go down steps into a hedged, unsurfaced lane where you go right to follow it into a field. Follow a tractor track down to pass right of a metal water trough and then cross a culverted stream up to a gate and stile. Continue forward with a hedge on your right up to another gate and stile.

If you wish to shorten your walk you can go right here to re-join the outward route and so return to the start.

However, to follow the whole of the walk – which is recommended – go forward and across a sloping field aiming for a pylon further ahead. This line will bring you to a fence near a stile above a stream. Cross the stile and immediately a second to then go over a footbridge and walk up the opposite bank to join the left hedge. Walking up the field with the hedge you will arrive in the top left corner where there is a stile. Go over and in five yards cross another on the right into the corner of a large sloping field.

Diagonally across the centre of the field you can see the buildings of Manor Abbey Farm. Head for these – a bearing of 290 degrees – and at the end of the field cross a stile near a gate. Joining a track go right with it and then follow the right hand hedge to a waymarked stile in the corner. Over the stile go straight across the field towards a lone oak tree.

To the left is the restored infirmary and a few fragments of wall belonging to

Halesowen Abbey. *While now under the wing of English Heritage – and watched over by the Halesowen Abbey Trust – access is still restricted to certain advertised dates.*

Just beyond the oak is another stile that you cross to turn sharp right with a hedge on the right.

➤ *Join the walk here if you are using public transport. At the end of your walk go forward to cross the stream and retrace your steps to the A456.*

You are now walking along an embankment forming one side of the ancient Abbey fish ponds.

Although now dry the ponds are still clearly visible and in medieval times were used to breed fish and thus provide fresh food. A little further on, in the fields to the left, you may be able to make out the line of the old Lapal Canal which with its notorious tunnel – over two miles long – was closed in 1917.

Stay with the hedge and embankment to bear right into a corner to a step stile. Go over it into a field and then left along the edge for 12 yards to steps on the left down to another stile. Cross the stile and its footbridge to continue along the bottom edge of the field with a stream on your left. This in turn brings you to another step stile in the corner over which you continue forward to a bottom corner where there is a stile and footpath signposts onto Lapal Lane South. Do not join the lane but turn right and go up with the edge of the field.

Pass the garden of a white house on the left to then reach a stile on the left just before the brow of the field.

Cross the stile into a hedged track and ignore the stile opposite to turn right through the wooden vehicle barrier posts and so follow the hedged path past a stile on the right to a junction of paths.

If you are using public transport go forward at this junction and continue reading from the third paragraph on page 17.

If you started from the car park in Lye Close Lane this junction is the one that you passed earlier. Here go left and up to the gate and stile leading onto the tarmac of Lye Close Lane and journey's end.

Magpie moth

Walk 6
Rolling Hills
Croxton

Some guide books dismiss Staffordshire as a flat and uninteresting county but, as with any sweeping statement, it doesn't take much effort to disprove the myth. This walk, which does exactly that, takes in two edges – or banks – and generally perambulates through rolling, picturesque countryside and woodland. Passing a cave and a stately home there is much of interest on this most enjoyable of walks – more than enough to silence the county's critics! But more of that later.

DISTANCE: 7¼ miles
MAPS: Landranger (1:50,000) 127
Pathfinder (1:25,000) 829
PARKING: Roadside in Croxton plus a small lay-by on the B5026 at GR 769336
START/FINISH: Bench seat near St. Paul's Church, Croxtonbank (GR 784325)

FROM the bench seat walk north-west along the unsurfaced lane at the side of the church and follow it down until meeting white 'Lilac Cottage' on the left. Here the main track swings left and you follow it for a few yards, to then turn right at a junction to follow a track up and right of another white cottage. Just past the cottage a waymarker post directs you into a hedged footpath on the edge of a field. Follow it for just a few yards and then cross a step stile into another field. In this field continue your line, now following a hedge/fence left, to pass between the hedge/ fence and a small pool. Continue with the hedge/fence down to a gate in the field corner.

Passing through the gate onto an unsurfaced farm track turn right to follow it for 45 yards to a T-junction with another track and a waymark arrow. Here turn left and follow this new track, which is in fact a hedged green lane, then bearing left as it passes a house with a very large pool behind it. Soon your way arrives at a gate into a field.

In the field and to your left you will see a nearby electricity pylon. Going left, pass between the pylon and the hedge to walk up the field to the top corner where there is a gateway and step stile. Cross the stile

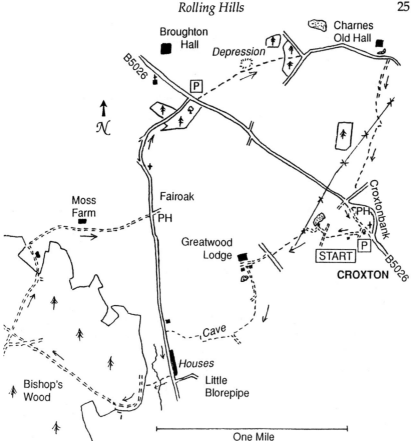

and, still following the hedge, walk up this field to the next corner where there is a step stile onto a surfaced lane.

Go right along the lane for 25 yds where you then turn left through the gate and onto the farm road to Greatwood Lodge. Follow the farm road to arrive at the farm buildings where you pass through two gates in quick succession. After the second gate you need to turn left through another gate to pass between two low stone barns and so arrive at yet another gate, with a waymark, next to a stone wall. Go through this gate and walk forward on the distinct track to follow the left-hand wall to a small pool where there is a marker post with an abundance of yellow waymark arrows.

Passing left of the pool continue forward on the track to meet two adjacent gates. Go through the right hand one to enter a large field where you continue your line, now with a hedge on your left. Near the top of the rise the vehicle track swings right but you continue forward with the left hedge until reaching the top corner where there is a double step stile next to a holly hedge. Cross and continue ahead with the hedge and fence on your left to the next corner.

Here there are two gates. Go through the left hand one into a track where immediately on the right there is a step stile – note the boundary stone next to it. Crossing the stile into a sloping field you now have a centre field crossing ahead of you. The line of your path is forward, on a bearing of 260 degrees, heading for a point between two large trees. On cresting the slope you will see a hedge and fence in front of you. Here you are on the ridge top where ahead and across the valley you can see the expanse of Bishop's Wood. As you approach the hedge and fence you will see that the wooden fence has a step. Cross the fence and now walk steeply down a small pasture with the hedge on your left to a step stile in the corner. In the next field go immediately right with the hedge on your right to the point where the hedge ends on a rock outcrop. Here your way is straight ahead for the 35 yards or so to the barbed wire fence in front.

Where the hedge ends at the rock outcrop a peek to the right and around the corner will reveal the cave marked on the Pathfinder map. The cave is however fenced and padlocked which suggests that it is private and/or dangerous. Please be guided accordingly.

Having arrived at the barbed wire fence now go left with it to pass an enamel bath doubling as a water trough, and so shortly arrive at a gap and gateway. Go through into another field where you walk forward a short way to join the protruding corner of a barbed wire fence. At the fence follow it as it swings right and then left to soon reach a gate onto a tarmac lane.

On the lane go left and follow it for about 400 yards to the last of a line of houses on the left. This last house has a post outside with the number '8' on it. It is also just before the turning for 'Little Blorepipe' – remember this name for later!

Opposite number 8 there is a step stile in the hedge. Go over it and walk very slightly left to cross the gated footbridge over the River Sow. Leaving the Sow to make its way to Stafford, you go forward to meet the left-hand fence. This short stretch can be muddy. At the fence go forward and up to meet a step stile into Bishop's Wood. Just a few yards after crossing the stile you meet the woodland perimeter track.

It was here I met an interesting 70 year old local who gave me the benefit of his knowledge. Seemingly the woodland belongs to the Church Commissioners who have let it to the Forestry Commission on a 999 year lease. At this point the trees are predominantly larch with a cosmetic curtain of spindly American oak.

Turning left along the perimeter track follow it as it swings right where after a while, and near a gate on the left, it strikes deeper into the trees and begins to rise in a generally north-westerly direction. Ignoring forestry tracks off left and right stay with your track for a further three-quarters of a mile until a larger, graded forestry road crosses in front of you. Go straight across on the smaller track opposite and in a short distance come to a cross road of tracks.

Now turn right to follow this new track as it rises and in a while emerges on the northern edge of the woods. Ahead a hunter's gate, with a yellow arrow on a red background awaits you and beyond it you can see the partly timbered Park House. But don't hurry – instead enjoy the fine view across the valley.

When you are ready to continue go through the hunter's gate and follow the hedged path down to a gate. Go through to pass left of Park House and then pass through a green gate. Now on a broad vehicle track follow it to the woodland corner where it swings right. Follow it right and down to another gate. On the other side follow the vehicle track forward, heading for Moss Farm. Immediately before the farm the track crosses a cattle grid and then becomes a hedged farm road as it passes right of the farm. Now follow this pleasant hedged farm road until it enters the hamlet of Fairoak at a road and almost opposite the 'Freemasons Arms'.

At the road turn left and rising, follow it for almost three-quarters of a mile to meet the B5026. Cross to the other side of the B5026 and turn right – signed Croxton and Eccleshall – for a distance of 55 yards where, before a white milestone, there is a wooden kissing gate on your left. Go through this and walk directly forward – 60 degrees – to pass immediately right of a fenced tree and so arrive at a ladder stile in the fence ahead.

To your left you can see the magnificent Broughton Hall. This timbered Elizabethan house, now a Franciscan Priory, was the scene of a dramatic Civil War episode involving that most famous of Stafford sons, Izaak Walton – author of the classic 'Compleat Angler'.

Following the Battle of Worcester a Royalist colonel sought refuge at Broughton Hall. With him he carried one of Charles II's crown jewels. The colonel, leaving the jewel with his host, left the hall and was subsequently arrested and incarcerated in the Tower of London. Walton, who was on one of his regular visits from London to his hometown, arranged to stay at nearby Blore Pipe House when he took possession of the jewel and carried it to London. The colonel then managed to escape from the Tower whereupon Walton gave the jewel to him so that he in turn could deliver it to Charles in France.

This is a delightful story of derring-do; carried out by a man in late middle-age who had never desired anything more exciting than landing a fish; – a good example of 'the time producing the man'!

Cross the ladder stile and in the next field follow the same direction – it was here I disturbed a February hare – aiming for what appears to be a gap in the stand of conifers ahead. Still in this field the line will bring you to a large, overgrown depression that you simply skirt to the right and so reach a step stile. Now in the third field your line is a bearing of 80 degrees ahead to the black metal kissing gate in the fence of the right-hand clump of trees. Arriving at the kissing gate go through it and forward along the broad grassy break through the trees. This will bring you to a gap in a hedge and stone steps down to the tarmac of a lane very near to a T-junction.

On the lane go right for the few feet to the junction and then turn left to follow the signs for Standon and Chatcull along another lane. Stay with this lane for almost half a mile to pass the remains of the moat around Charnes Old Hall where on the right, and opposite the gable ends of barns, there is a double metal gate with a public footpath waymark. Go through and enter what very quickly becomes a hedged green lane. Soon arriving at another double metal gate with a step stile enter the next field to walk up the clear vehicle track with the hedge and fence on your right. At the top corner you will be faced with three wooden gates, each with a hunter's gate at the side. The left hand gate has a step stile. Cross the stile and immediately swing right along a grassy vehicle track to follow the right hand hedge up towards overhead power lines. About 75 yards after passing under the power lines you will come to a large gap in the top corner hedge.

Through the gap and instantly on the right there is a stile step in a section of wooden fence. Cross it and go left to follow the fence on the left and with the power lines to your right. Keeping the fence on your left follow it down the field where, just before the corner and on the left next to a tree, you will see a fence stile. DO NOT CROSS THIS ONE. Instead continue following the fence for another 35 yards to the corner where a step stile awaits you.

Cross over this one and go left down between a hedge and fence for just a few yards to enter a field corner. To your right, in the corner, is a wide gap in the hedge. Going through it your path now crosses this next field on a line just left of the pub seen in the distance. This is a bearing of 200 degrees and at the time of writing there was a tractor trail marking the line.

By following this line across and down the field you will come to a step stile onto a narrow metalled lane. Turn right along the lane to meet the B5026 again. To your left is 'The Vernon Yonge Arms' pub and next to it a telephone kiosk and letter box. Go to the telephone kiosk and pass right of it and the pub to walk up a green lane that a short way in carries a waymark sign. Soon it becomes a hedged footpath and leads you through an ornamental metal kissing gate. Continue forward with a fence on your left to pass right of a small pool and so reach another metal kissing gate. Through this go the few yards forward to the corner of the track ahead and the white 'Lilac Cottage' of your outward journey.

Now just walk forward and up to arrive back at the church and your starting point.

Shire foal

Walk 7
From Edge to Dale
Munslow

Munslow is another of those small Shropshire villages that straddle the B4368 Morville to Craven Arms road. Below Middlehope Hill and in the attractive Corve Dale, the present day village is now a quiet black and white backwater. However the Crown Inn – a former hundred house – plus a fine Norman church with fourteenth century stained glass, give testimony to its past importance. It once had a motte and bailey castle but the motte was levelled in the eighteenth century.

With Munslow at the start and finish, this walk enjoys outstanding hilltop views to Wenlock Edge and also across Corve Dale to the Clee Hills.

DISTANCE: 7½ miles
MAPS: Landranger (1:50,000) 137
Pathfinder (1:25,000) 931
PARKING: Roadside in Munslow or lay-by just south-west of Aston Munslow. If using this latter parking place then start the walk from The Swan.
PUBLIC TRANSPORT: Very limited service from Bridgnorth. An early morning bus will take you to Tugford with a convenient return at tea-time. From Tugford walk south-west to Broncroft Lodge (see Landranger map 137) and pick up the walk from there. This will add about 4½ miles to the walk. Midland Red West Service 715 (Mon. - Fri.)
START/FINISH: War Memorial Munslow (GR 522874)

FROM the village War Memorial, at the junction with the B4368, take the signed no through road – also signed for Munslow Church – and follow it uphill and through a right bend to a junction where there is a roadside mirror. Here turn left to pass the church where, immediately beyond the church, the tarmac swings left and on the right of the bend there is a bridleway sign in front of a house and next to a gate. Follow the sign through the gate and in 25 yards – just before another gate – bear left and walk up the now sunken track. Stay with this way as it rises – notice the layered limestone rock formations – to reach a gate and step stile. Cross over and go forward to pass through

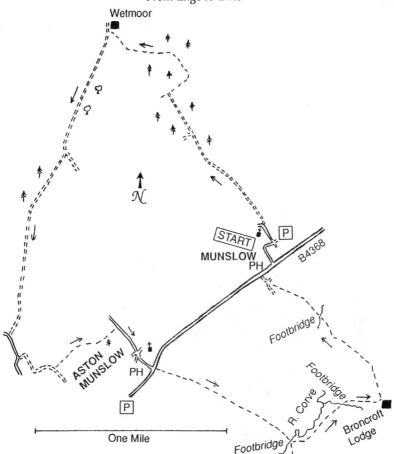

the gate immediately opposite and so enter an attractive, hedged green lane.

Continuing to rise, follow the green lane where in a while the right hand hedge gives way to woodland. Further along a bridleway comes in from the left but you stay with your track, still rising, now with trees on both sides. Passing another track on the left you will eventually come to something of a clearing at the top of the slope. This is in effect a T-junction with a broad cross track. Here go right and follow the broad track between the trees and stay with it as it veers left and begins a gentle descent. Soon the descent steepens and your track is now on the edge of an embankment to the right. Ignoring a right turn down the embankment stay with your main track where in a while the woodland ends on the right. Further on you will meet a wooden gate through which you completely leave the woodland to follow the right hand fence forward to a gate immediately left of Wetmoor Farm.

Go through this gate and turn immediately left to follow a fence on the left and a line of trees on the right, up to another gate. Through the gate continue forward with the clear track to reach the upper field corner where you go through a hunter's gate to follow the right hand hedge in the next field. Walk up this field to the top corner where you will meet woodland and another hunter's gate. Pass through and now follow the rising track along the bottom edge of the woodland with outstanding views to the right across Wenlock Edge and the Shropshire Hills. At the top the track swings left and out of the trees where you will meet a track junction. Turn right to follow a broad track with woodland on the right and a hedge on the left.

Middlehope Hill

Now follows a mile of excellent walking with far ranging views across Corve Dale to the Clee Hills.

Stay with this track, ignoring a branch that goes right into the trees and down the hillside. After a while, and at the end of the woodland, your track becomes hedged on both sides. Now follow it all the way to a metalled lane where you turn left. Walk along the lane for about 200 yards to a bend where a track goes right and a hedged green lane goes left. Turn left and follow the green lane as it swings right, and then in a while left, and then in a further while right and right again. On this last bend there is a fence stile on the left into a field.

Go over the stile and in the field walk forward with the right hand hedge to arrive at a corner. In the very corner there is a step stile that takes you into a large pasture. Here go slightly right to pass right of a stone barn and then head for a telegraph pole behind a hedge and fence. Arriving at the hedge, fence and a gate, swing left to now follow the edge of a small coppice, keeping it on your right. Go through a gate and so continue following the coppice and the field edge to then meet a surfaced lane.

On the lane go right and downhill to pass the White House – a fourteenth century manor – and so reach the Swan – a historic inn – next to the B4368.

After perhaps taking refreshments, cross the B4368 to the signed public footpath opposite. Enter the hedged track – which can be muddy for a short way – and follow it to reach a pole fence that you cross to continue the short way into a narrow pasture. Here walk forward through the centre of the field where in the far fence you will see a stile near to a gate. In the next field follow the same line across the centre to arrive at another stile and gate half way along the opposite hedge.

Cross the stile and again following the same line make for yet another stile between two trees and just past a protruding hedge corner. On arrival you will see that it is in fact a double stile into a narrow pasture. Cross the narrow pasture to the stile in the opposite corner and so enter a very large field. Follow the same line, aiming right of a line of trees, to the substantial footbridge you can see ahead that crosses the River Corve. This is a tranquil spot and a truly pastoral scene.

On the opposite bank turn left and walk the short distance to a wooden fence next to the river. Cross over into a field and go straight ahead to cut the corner and so reach the bank again on a sharp U-bend in the river. Now leave the bank again to follow a line of 45 degrees across the field – as the river meanders to your left – to reach a gate in the hedge ahead. *If the way is cropped and the path not clear you can always follow the river bank to the same point.* Through the gate follow the same line across the next field to the far corner where there is a footbridge over a tributary of the Corve.

At the time of writing this footbridge was not in a good state of repair though it was negotiable. The need for repair has been reported to the County Council and may have been carried out by the time you walk the route. In any event there are several points where the stream can be jumped or forded.

On the opposite bank walk the few yards to the gate ahead and enter a field. Follow the bank of the stream for approximately 60 yards to a small bend. From here you will see the buildings of Broncroft Lodge Farm. Now go diagonally across the field aiming for the corner immediately left of the farm buildings. On arrival at the corner you will find a gate that you go through into another field. Here go right along the edge of the field for 25 yards to a wide gap in the hedge, in front of outbuildings. Now with your back to the outbuildings face out across the field and walk across it – half right – on a bearing of 350 degrees and aiming for the left hand of two trees in the hedgerow. This line will bring you to an old wooden gate next to the tree. Go over, through or around the gate into the corner of the next field.

From here you face another field crossing, this time on a bearing of 310 degrees that will bring you to the furthest corner. Here you will find a gap and a culverted ditch. Cross over and follow the right hand hedge and fence for about 50 yards to an inverted corner at the side of the River Corve. In the corner and to your right is a pole fence that you cross to follow the river bank upstream until soon meeting another substantial footbridge.

NB. These two field crossings require some care for there is a shortage of readily identifiable landmarks. If you do go astray it is well to remember that the general line between Broncroft Lodge and the river footbridge is north-westerly.

Cross over and on the other side go half right on a bearing of 320 degrees. Follow this line until meeting a hedge where you turn left to follow it to a fence stile in the field corner. In the next field continue forward with the hedge and fence on your right to arrive at a gate and fence stile at the top. Crossing the stile you enter a hedged green lane at a junction. Go straight ahead up to the B4368 and The Crown – the hundred house – where a right turn for a few yards brings you back to the War Memorial.

*Great spotted
woodpecker*

Walk 8
The Muchness of Wenlock
Much Wenlock

Much Wenlock is an ancient little market town that, historically, has it all. Based on the Priory ruins – the monastery of St. Milburgha was founded as early as the seventh century – the town has that original quality that many better known places aspire to, but rarely attain. The town guide leaflet, obtainable from the museum and information office, contains twenty-two places of interest yet, with the best will in the world, still cannot cover all the town's facets. Beware! – if you are not careful you can spend all day in Much Wenlock and forget your walk which also takes in the National Trust's imposing Benthall Hall.

DISTANCE: 8½ miles
MAPS: Landranger (1:50,000) 127
Pathfinder (1:25,000) 890 & 911
PARKING: Public Car Parks in Much Wenlock
PUBLIC TRANSPORT: Midland Red West Service 436/437 Shrewsbury
- Bridgnorth. Alight at Much Wenlock.
START/FINISH: Town Centre, Much Wenlock (GR 623000)

S O, leaving the town centre, follow the signs for Wenlock Priory along the Bull Ring to pass the entrance and car park. Beyond is a 'no through road' sign that you follow to leave the town on this surfaced lane. In a while it swings right to pass the entrance to the Severn-Trent water treatment plant and then left to a gate onto the drive to Downsmill – note the Shropshire Way buzzard symbol. Follow the drive to arrive at the front of the converted mill.

Pass through the gate on the right of the house to follow the garden wall for the short distance to a footbridge. On the other side of the stream go half left over the brow of the field to a gate and stile. In the next field continue forward with the hedge on your left to another stile that gives access into a hedged track and so to another gate and stile onto the tarmac lane in front of Bradley Farm.

Cross over the lane and enter the farmyard, to then turn left to the front of the farmhouse. Here turn right to pass between the farm outbuildings to a gate ahead bearing a yellow waymark and a 'buzzard'. Enter the field and cross it half left (55 degrees) to a point half way along the opposite hedge. At the hedge turn left to follow it – on your right – to the field corner where there is another stile. Cross it and continue forward with the hedge on your right and walk down towards the field corner. Before the corner be alert for a wooden wicket gate on the right and in a dip. Go through this and up the other side into a field.

Unfortunately in this field several hedges have been removed making path finding a little difficult. While the right of way heads across the crops to an oak tree in the middle, the problem is easily, and practically, overcome by turning left to follow the field boundary in a clockwise direction. At the first corner go right – with the hedge on your left – and

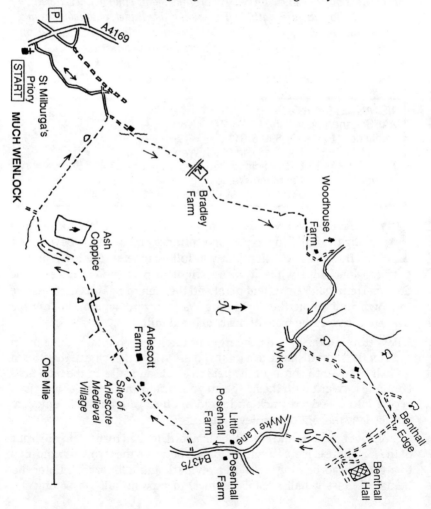

A fine timber framed building in Much Wenlock

half way along pass a stile and gate. Continue following the hedge – you are now back on the proper footpath – to a corner where a gateway leads you into a hedged track that passes below Woodhouse Farm and then joins its drive. Bear right to follow the track/drive through woodland to a T-junction with a tarmac lane.

Turn right along this quiet, wooded lane – so quiet that I disturbed rabbits and squirrels on the tarmac – and follow it for half a mile towards the tiny hamlet of Wyke. At the top of a rise pass a T-junction and go left to a sharp right bend. On the left of the bend is a wooden footpath sign inscribed 'Shropshire Way' and pointing down a track that also carries a sign 'Private Road'.

Follow the track down, and then up, to pass right of Cowslip Cottage and so into a field. In the field go slightly left to a barbed wire fence and follow it forward to the field corner and so through a waymarked gap into the next field. Follow the left hedge of this second field to a stile in the corner that takes you into the woods on Benthall Edge.

Benthall Edge is a tree clad escarpment overlooking the River Severn and the Ironbridge Gorge. Not a great deal can be seen of the valley floor due to tree

*cover, but this is no great loss as below you is the mighty Ironbridge Power
Station!*

In the woods walk along the clear path that in a short while begins to
descend and then joins a trackway on a hairpin bend. Take the upper
arm of the hairpin and rise with the track as it then swings right to a gate
and stile. Cross the stile and walk along the hedged track – ignore the
joining track left – for a little less than half a mile to pass immediately
right of Benthall Hall Farm. Just beyond the farm is a public footpath

Benthall Hall

sign and stile on the right. If you don't wish to view Benthall Hall, then
cross this stile and read from ➡ (p.39).

To see Benthall Hall continue past the footpath sign and stile to meet
the junction with 'The Avenue' that gives entry to the Hall and its church.
Opposite this junction is a gate giving access to a public footpath which,
if you follow it for a short distance, will give you a view of the Hall's
impressive frontage.

*Home of the Benthall family this distinguished stone building is one of the
lesser known National Trust properties. It possesses an intricately carved oak
staircase with oak panelling and an elaborately decorated ceiling. It is open to
the public from 1.30 to 5.30pm on Wednesdays, Sundays and Bank Holiday
Mondays from 31 March to the end of September – but check before visiting as
dates and times can change (tel: 0952-882159). The attractive church has some
unusual features, including a sun dial set in the wall.*

To continue your walk retrace your steps back to the public footpath
sign and stile near Benthall Hall Farm and go left over the stile.

➡ In the field go forward and down with the hedge on your left to the field corner. Ahead you can see the scar of a quarry. In the corner go over the stile at the side of a gate and continue with the left hedge to its protruding corner. Here go half left – due south – to cut one corner and meet yet another protruding corner. At this second protrusion continue on the same line with the hedge on your left and a pool, containing some waterfowl, on your right. Continue with this strip of field as it narrows to a gate and stile leading onto a hedged path. Follow this to a tarmac lane where you turn left to a T-junction with the B4375. Here turn right – signed for Much Wenlock and Shrewsbury – and passing Little Posen-

hall Farm on the right and Posenhall Farm on the left arrive at a public footpath sign on the right, just before a right bend in the road.

Turn right into this hedged footpath and follow it to a stile into a field. With the hedge on the left continue on the same line along this large field where, just before the corner, you will see a stile on the left. Cross the stile and turn immediately right to follow your previous line – but on the other side of the hedge – for the few yards to the corner and another stile.

Over this stile continue forward and down to pass left of Arlescott Cottage and into the bottom corner of the field. In the corner drop down to go through a wooden

Benthall church and sundial

hunter's gate that takes you into pasture. On your left is a fence surrounding a pool. Follow the fence forward, leaving it as it goes left, and follow the same line across the pasture – left of Arlescott Farm – to the corner with a gate and two stiles. *According to the Ordnance Survey map this last pasture contains the site of Arlescott Medieval Village.*

Crossing the two stiles onto a cross track your way lies straight ahead across a field to a protruding hedge corner – this is your next objective. Walk across the centre of the field (a bearing of 240 degrees) to the hedge corner that is right of a gap in the hedge.

Alternatively, if the way is obstructed by crops, follow the field boundary clockwise to the same point.

At the corner go forward on the same line so as to keep the hedge on your left to the top left corner of the field where there is another gap in the hedge near the stump of a sawn-off tree. Go left through the gap and immediately right to a stile in the corner. To your left, in the hedge, is a white triangulation pillar standing at 751 feet.

Over the stile continue on the same line now with the hedge on your right. To your left are the Clee Hills and to the right is the Wrekin. In the next corner drop down into a hedged path and follow it down over two stiles to shortly enter a shallow valley. Following the bottom of the valley you will see a stile and gate ahead. This gives access to a pasture that you walk down keeping close to the right hand fence.

In a short while you will make out the shape of a watercourse on your left. Keep between the watercourse and the right hand fence to the bottom of the pasture where you DO NOT go through the gateway but instead follow the fence left to the watercourse itself and a stile. Over the stile turn immediately left to walk between a fence left and a field boundary right and so arrive at two stiles.

Go over the right hand stile into the field and forward with the hedge left. In the next field corner another waymarked stile awaits you. Cross it and go half right towards a pool and pass to the right of it. Ahead and across the valley you can see the remains of a windmill. Towards the bottom of this field bear right with the right hand hedge to cross a culverted stream where immediately left you will see a stile and gate. Cross the stile into the lane, by the gate to Downsmill, that you walked on your outward journey.

Now turning left along the lane just retrace your way back to Much Wenlock and its antiquities.

Walk 9
An Urban Interlude
Trysull

It comes as something of a surprise to find such attractive landscapes immediately on the western boundary of Wolverhampton. Indeed at one point this walk is within two miles of the town boundary yet you will see little or no evidence of that fact, surrounded as you are by a charming rural scene.

DISTANCE: 9 miles
MAPS: Landranger (1:50,000) 138 & 139
Pathfinder (1:25,000) 912
PARKING: Roadside, Trysull
PUBLIC TRANSPORT: Midland Red West Service 585/586/587 from Wolverhampton to Trysull.
START/FINISH: All Saints Church, Trysull (GR 852943)

FROM the parish church walk along The Holloway, signed for Merry Hill and Wolverhampton. Soon cross the Smestow Brook – which will be a recurring companion throughout this walk – and in a few yards turn left along the waymarked bridleway to pass the old mill. Rising a little, the track continues for three quarters of a mile until meeting a road at Seisdon. Here go left and then turn right along Post Office Road and follow it until you arrive at the entrance to Seisdon House where adjacent to the wall is a public footpath and Staffordshire Way sign.

The Staffordshire Way is an outstanding long distance footpath, created by Staffordshire County Council, that extends over 90 miles from Mow Cop on the northern border with Cheshire to Kinver Edge on the southern border with Worcestershire. It is waymarked throughout with signposts and arrow symbols containing the celebrated Staffordshire Knot.

Go right with the sign and along the surfaced path that gradually ascends to a low hilltop. At the top the path has widened to a track where, near a partly concealed treatment plant, it then makes a sharp right bend. This is where you leave the track to continue ahead with the Staffordshire Way. On the left, and on the bend, is a gateway and step stile after which you then go immediately left through a metal gate. On the other side of the gate, and immediately on your right, is a way-

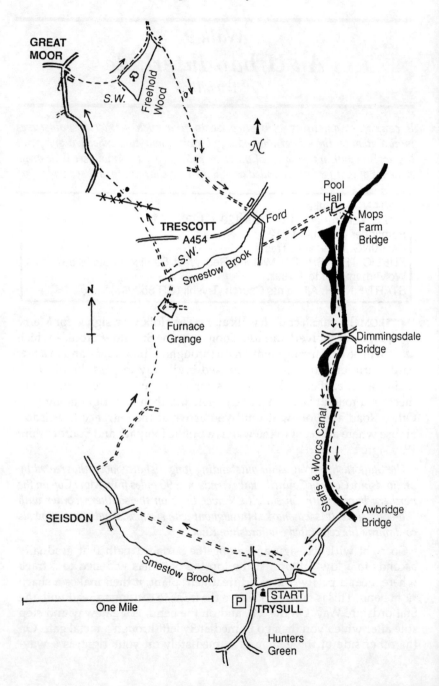

A peaceful scene on the Staffs. & Worcs. canal

marked stile that you go over to then walk forward to another stile that is accompanied by a signpost. Walk across the middle of the large pasture to the far hedge and fence where, slightly right of centre, you will come to a double stile.

Cross it and the one immediately ahead to follow the direction of another signpost across the field – the path, being the Staffordshire Way, is well trodden – to a stile and gate. In the next field follow the left hedge to another gate into the large open yard of Furnace Grange Farm. Here take the farm drive that goes slightly left towards the main road. In a short while cross the Smestow Brook just beyond which a waymark on the right takes the Staffordshire Way towards Trescott. This is where you leave the long distance path to stay with the farm drive and reach the A454.

This is a very busy road so take care as you cross and enter a field through a gap almost opposite. Walk up the gently sloping field with a hedge on your right. At the top views extend left to the Clee Hills and half right to the Perton Ridge. Pass under the overhead power lines to enter a second field where again you follow the right-hand hedge almost to its protruding corner and a pool.

Your way now leaves this point to go left across the field on a bearing of 310 degrees, aiming just left of some farm buildings, to meet a step stile and footpath sign in the opposite hedge and on the bend of an unsurfaced lane. Should the line be obstructed with crops you may need to follow the field edge to the same point.

Now head forward (north) along this splendid traffic-free lane, part of which is a ford, until reaching the junction of lanes and the culverted stream at secluded Great Moor. To your right is a public footpath sign for 'Trescott 1¼'. Go right with the sign and along the farm road to keep the farm buildings on your right.

At the end of the buildings you face two gates leading into fields. Take the left one onto a clear track forward and below an embankment. In a short way and on flat ground you will meet a hedge that you keep on your left as you walk to and through a gate. Continue with the hedge and then where it ends just keep forward for a few yards to the corner of Freehold Wood. Here you meet the Staffordshire Way again and to the right is a wooden footbridge with the familiar waymark. Do not cross it but instead turn left and keep the wood on your right to follow its edge all the way to a stile and signpost. Again do not follow the Staffordshire Way arrows but turn right on a broad track along the other edge of the wood. Ignoring a first left turn continue forward to the end of the woodland where on your right you will see a narrow gateway. Pass through it and turn immediately left to follow the same line but with the hedge on your left and parallel to your original broad track. Passing through several fields, still with the hedge on your left, continue forward to then meet another track at a T-junction. Turn left and follow this clear way to houses on the A454.

Opposite is a lane with a 'Ford' sign. Follow it and cross your old friend the Smestow Brook by using the footbridge at the side of the ford. Rounding the right bend continue along the lane until, just past a house on the left, you will find the entrance to a 'Road Used as a Public Path' (RUPP). Turn left along the RUPP which although narrow and largely unsurfaced is well used by fishermen's cars on their way to, or from, the reservoirs. Following it beyond the fishermen's turn-off continue towards Pool Hall Farm and at the first barn go right with the track and then left to arrive directly in front of the farmhouse. Pass right of the farmhouse to the canal bridge and descend to the towpath where you go right (south) along the attractive Staffordshire and Worcestershire Canal. To your right are the canal feeder reservoirs with their many waterfowl. Pass under Dimmingsdale Bridge (No. 53) and then at Dimmingsdale Lock the towpath changes to the opposite bank – this takes you past Ebstree Lock and in a while arrives at Awbridge Bridge (No. 49).

Leave the canal here and go right along the road as far as an acute left bend. Leaving the road in the corner, and following the direction of the waymark sign, enter a field to follow the right hand hedge. In a short distance the hedge goes right and you continue forward across the field to a telegraph pole left of an electricity pylon. At the field crest the path falls away towards a white house. Follow it to the bottom field corner but do not join the road, instead turn right through 90 degrees and follow a left-hand hedge for about 25 yards to a waymarked stile. Cross the stile and walk forward with, yes, the Smestow Brook on your left and the slopes of the imaginatively named 'The Grotto' on your right. Coming to a gate and stile cross over and follow the shady track forward to meet the road at the side of a farm.

Turn left along the road and cross the Smestow back to your starting point at Trysull church.

Badger

Walk 10
The Lost Village
Nordy Bank

It's strange, but true, that some of the paths on this walk are shown as bridleways – both on Ordnance Survey maps and on signs erected by the County Council – yet the only access to them is by a stile!

In high summer one short section can be quite overgrown making the full walk a little strenuous – hence the variation in distance. Nonetheless it really is rural South Shropshire at its best for, not only does it take in two important historic landmarks, it offers quite outstanding landscapes.

DISTANCE: 9 or 6¾ miles
MAPS: Landranger (1:50,000) 137
Pathfinder (1:25,000) 931
PARKING: Nordy Bank Common
PUBLIC TRANSPORT: Very limited service from Bridgnorth. An early morning bus will take you to Tugford (where you can pick up the route from the point marked ➤ on page 51) with a convenient return at tea-time. Midland Red West Service 715 (Mon. - Fri.)
START/FINISH: Nordy Bank Common (GR 572850)

A T a very convenient off road parking area below Nordy Bank hill fort you will see a litter bin, a letter box for Laburnum Cottage, and a gate that gives access to the bottom edge of Nordy Bank Common. This is the start of your walk.

Go through the gate and follow the right hand fence and its line of trees as it descends and then swings right to another gate that takes you off the common and on to a track. Follow the track down to houses and the service track in front of them. In front of the houses turn left to go through a gate and then, passing a drive with a cattle grid on the left, continue forward to enter the yard of Marsh Farm. Keep left of the farmhouse and continue forward to pass close to stables and so meet a hedged green lane. Follow the hedged lane forward and down to a small stream which you cross. Now follow the lane up and onwards, passing a track that goes right, and then pass a small stone building – also on the right. From here the way becomes rather more sunken and passes

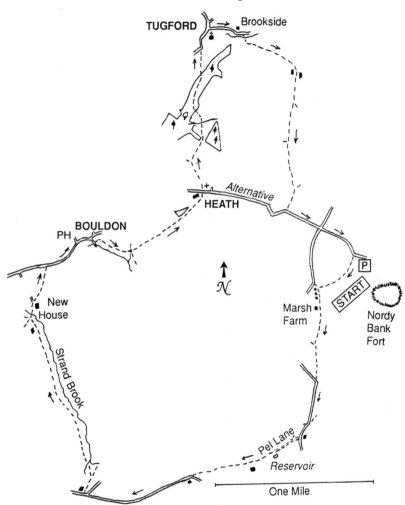

between holly trees, then to rise to meet a metalled lane at Nordy Bank Nurseries.

Turn left along the lane and follow it steeply up to the top where on the left a gate with two letter boxes gives access onto heathland. You, however, continue forward with the lane, as it swings right and then left, to arrive at the entrance to a track on the right, just past a white house on the left. Go right into the unsurfaced track which is known as Pel Lane and follow it, soon to swing left. Continue with it as the track follows the top of what is effectively a broad ridge. There are superb views to the Clees left and across Corve Dale to the Long Mynd right.

Passing just right of a covered reservoir your track comes to a gate. Go through and now follow the right hand hedge on the same line to pass, via a series of gates, through pasture and paddock keeping well right of, and above, a farm. Arriving at a large, sloping field enter it and stay with the right hand hedge as views now really open out. In a while you will reach the top far corner where a final gate takes you onto a surfaced lane at a bend.

Turn right along the lane – Scirmidge Lane – and follow it down to pass a wind pump on the right. After half a mile along this lane you will come to a Give Way sign at Red Furlongs. At the junction go forward along the road signed for Ludlow and in only a few yards go right over the stile at the side of the cottage wall. In the field go down with the hedge on your left to follow it as it swings left, descending almost to the very bottom corner of the field. Just before the bottom, and on the left, you will see a waymarked step stile in the fence – behind a small pool. Cross the stile and the infant Strand Brook to swing right so as to follow the brook downstream on the left bank.

Now staying with the brook as the valley narrows slightly, cross the bottom edge of several fields by a series of waymarked stiles – always keeping the stream on your right. After a while the sides of the valley gradually open out and you enter a long pasture where your brook-side route takes you, below a stand of trees, to a gate.

Here you go through and follow a grassy track forward between hedgerows – still with the stream on your right – that will bring you to a cottage. Pass to the right of the cottage along a green lane and reach a gate. Through the gate turn immediately right to cross the bridge over your old friend the Strand Brook. Rising into a field you will see a gate in the hedge opposite, near the corner. Walk to it and then turn left, with the hedge and fence on your right, to follow the faint vehicle track towards New House Farm. Arriving at the field corner go through the gate on the right into the farmyard and then turn left for a few yards to the end of the farm buildings. Ahead of you is the gate to the main farm drive that leads to the road and to the right of this is another gate at the corner of a barn that leads into a field.

Go through the right hand gate and in the field walk half right across the slope aiming for the opposite hedge and a gate halfway along it next to two trees – which in turn are near a water trough. At the gate go through into another field and cross it to the furthermost right hand corner where there is a stile onto the road.

Join the road and turn right towards Bouldon. On the way pass the Tally Ho pub which, like any good country inn, has a public footpath sign pointing to it. Continue along the road into the village and where the road swings sharp left near a telephone kiosk you go straight ahead along the signed No Through Road. Immediately before a stone bridge go left through the gate of a signed bridleway where you then take the right hand of the two gates facing you. Going right follow the field bottom and just before the field corner, in a slight dip, go through the gate in the right

Decorated doorway at Heath Chapel

hand hedge. Now turn immediately left and follow the same line with the hedge now on your left. Ignoring a gate on the left continue forward and down to a gate immediately before a small stream, which can be dry!

Go through the gate to cross the stream and then turn left up to another gate. Through this, turn instantly right to follow the hedge and fence up the steep bank. As soon as possible change to the other side of the hedge and fence – there are several gaps – and follow it up to the top corner of the pasture where there is a fence stile. Cross it and continue upwards now with a fence on your right to the top corner of the field where there is a gate. Through the gate carry on the same line upwards, now with the fence and hedge on your left, to pass through the remains of a field boundary and then right of a stand of trees.

Stay with the hedge and fence to the top of the slope to arrive at the corner of a wall next to a farm. At the corner there is a gate on the left that you go through to immediately swing right across the edge of the farmyard and through a gate out of it. On the other side of the gate go left to follow the few yards of partly broken wall to the stile onto the lane.

This lane is the demarcation point referred to in the introduction. Should it be high summer and you are not keen on nettles and brambles (or do not have a stick) then go right (east) along the lane and follow it all the way back to Nordy Bank – see sketch map – but do have a look at Heath Chapel first. If however it is late autumn, winter or early spring and you are still feeling energetic then continue from the next paragraph.

Cross the narrow lane where directly opposite is another bridleway sign partly hidden in the hedge. Next to it is a metal hurdle gate that you cross into a field containing the ancient Heath Chapel.

Here in fact you are at the centre of the lost medieval village of Heath and the stone chapel is its sole survivor, a remarkable building dating from 1090 and still looking pretty much as it must have done when first built. Spend some time exploring this unique piece of history with its fine Norman door arch and its priceless, partly concealed, wall paintings. Over the centuries these have been covered by whitewash and now await the expertise – and the funds – to uncover them. Sufficient can be made out of St. George slaying the dragon and, on the opposite wall, the Ten Commandments.

Leaving the chapel, continue across the field to the corner near the small graveyard where there is a cross pole. Go over, or under, the pole and in the next field head for the protruding corner of a hedge opposite. On the way to it you will see the mounds and depressions that are all that remain of the village. At the hedge continue forward with the hedge on your right to another protruding corner where you go right, around the corner, to follow the ditch to a solitary wooden hunter's gate in the field corner.

Pass through the gate and initially following the right hand hedge aim for the left hand corner of the stand of trees ahead. Where your hedge swings right go ahead for the few yards to a line of three trees. At the first tree go slightly left for the short distance to the upper end of the remains of a hedge containing a partially hidden concrete water trough. Here you are just a short distance from, and adjacent to, the corner of the stand of trees.

Now cross the middle of the next sloping field, again slightly left and on a bearing of due north, to arrive at a gate that is above a deep gully. Go through the gate and immediately over the culvert leave the broad track to go right up an embankment, with a fence, then to leave the fence after about 35 yards and drop down the sloping field on a bearing of 315 degrees to a hunter's gate in an inverted corner of the fence around Tugford Coppice.

Go through the hunter's gate into the coppice and follow the clear path that descends to another hunter's gate in the bottom edge. Pass through the gate and follow the right hand hedge down the side of the field to a stile onto the road at the edge of Tugford village. Turn right along the road and follow it through the village.

➤ *Start and end your walk here if you are using public transport.*

Just before a junction with signposts, there is a white gate on the right with a sign inviting you 'To the Church'. At the junction go right along the lane signed for Abdon to pass a telephone kiosk and in a while arrive at Brookside Cottage on the left. About 35 yards beyond Brookside Cottage you will find a small wooden gate on the right that gives access to a substantial footbridge.

Cross the bridge and go forward up a bank and then swing left to a gap entrance into a sloping field. In the field bear left and follow the bottom boundary to pass through a gateway. In this next field gradually leave the bottom boundary and walk across the slope on a bearing of 120 degrees to pass right of an old gnarled oak. Ahead is a wire fence where the top strand of barbed wire has been removed and immediately behind it is a fence stile. Cross both and go forward with trees on your right to cross the rough pasture and then meet the remains of a hedge. Follow the hedge forward, keeping it on your right, to a corner where you now cross a wooden fence. On the other side still follow the right hand hedge up and forward – you can see the top of a chimney ahead – to another field corner where there is a gate.

Go through the gate and shortly across a tarmac drive, just below the buildings of Lower Norncott Farm, and then walk to the far corner of a black barn bearing the makers plate 'F H Dale. Builder. Leominster'. From this corner go the few yards to the hedge in front where with just a little exploration you will find a wooden hunter's gate.

Pass through into an open green space above a house and cross up to a black metal gate near the farm buildings that leads into a field. Through this follow the farm track forward, above an embankment and trees to the left. As it leaves the embankment and trees the track becomes a little fainter and then progresses parallel to a fence left. Arriving in a field corner the farm track then goes through a wide gap left and into a sloping field. Your path however, which is now a bridleway, goes forward and slightly right along a sunken and hedged green lane.

All too soon the left hand hedge disappears and you continue forward with the right hand hedge to a gate on the right. Passing through the gate continue forward in the same direction but now with the hedge on your left. Just before the top corner of this field you will pass a gate in the hedge and just beyond that your hedged bridleway reappears. Follow the hedged track forward where, for a short way, it can be somewhat overgrown in high summer. Stay with it until reaching an old metal gate across the way. On the other side a broad gravel track comes in from the left and your way continues forward along it for some easy walking. In a while go through a gate across the track and follow it as it swings right to then meet a tarmac lane.

Turn left at the lane and follow it downhill to crossroads. Ahead you can see the ramparts of Nordy Bank hill fort and journeys end. At the crossroads go over and follow the lane signed for Cockshutford up the hill and so back to your start at Nordy Bank Common.

Before your journey home do have a look at the substantial ditch and dyke at Nordy Bank, the best preserved of the Iron Age hill forts on Brown Clee. Inside, the short springy turf is a delight!

Yew

Walk 11
All Around The Wrekin
The Wrekin

A book of ridge and valley walks in the Midlands would be incomplete without a walk over the Wrekin. Perhaps the most famous of all Midland landmarks – and certainly one of the most visited – comparatively little has been written about it despite it having several facets, not least being the ancient hill fort on the summit.

This whaleback, that marks the division between Shropshire Plain, Shropshire Hills and Industrial Shropshire, was once a volcano. Its dramatic rock outcrops give ample testimony of past lava flows. Totally dominating the surrounding countryside it is easy to see why it became the site for a hill fort. Even today its military connections continue – there is a firing range located on the north-west flank; but fear not!, you will be safe if you stay with the described route.

Curiously, at the north-eastern end of the hill fort, the outer and inner gateways are named Hell Gate and Heaven Gate!

DISTANCE: 9 miles
MAPS: Landranger (1:50,000) 126 & 127
Pathfinder (1:25,000) 889 & 890
PARKING: Roadside at cross roads on B4380. Limited roadside in Eaton Constantine and limited roadside in Spout Lane.
PUBLIC TRANSPORT: Midland Red West Service 436/437 Shrewsbury - Bridgnorth. Alight at Cressage and walk north along the B4380 for about one mile to the cross roads
START/FINISH: B4380 cross roads south of Eaton Constantine (GR 596058)

FROM the cross roads walk northwards to reach the edge of Eaton Constantine village. Bear right with the road to pass right of St. Mary's parish church and then, after some interesting old buildings, past a Post Office letter box and a telephone kiosk before arriving at Garmston Lane on the right.

Turn right with the sign for Garmston and follow the lane to and through the hamlet, passing the lane junctions with Bennetts Lane and The Rudge; both on the right. Continue with Garmston Lane until arriving at a bridleway sign on the left, just before Garmston Farm and

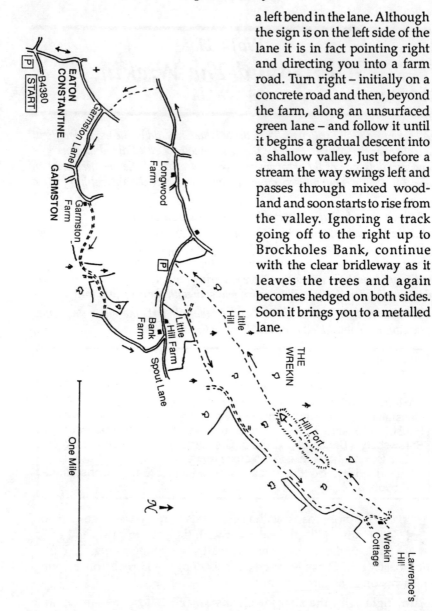

a left bend in the lane. Although the sign is on the left side of the lane it is in fact pointing right and directing you into a farm road. Turn right – initially on a concrete road and then, beyond the farm, along an unsurfaced green lane – and follow it until it begins a gradual descent into a shallow valley. Just before a stream the way swings left and passes through mixed woodland and soon starts to rise from the valley. Ignoring a track going off to the right up to Brockholes Bank, continue with the clear bridleway as it leaves the trees and again becomes hedged on both sides. Soon it brings you to a metalled lane.

At the lane turn left and follow it for almost half a mile to a T-junction with Spout Lane. Turn left along Spout Lane passing the white Bank Farm on the left and Little Hill Farm on the right. In a further 450 yards you will arrive at a double wooden gate on the right, set back from the lane and with a not too obvious public footpath sign.

Go through the gates and forward on a broad track. On the right a sign, high in a tree, states 'Raby Estate – Private Woods'. Follow the broad track – ignoring crossing tracks – as it quickly swings right and rises gently through the trees. After a while your path will bring you to the woodland edge where on your right is a pasture and beyond it the white Bank Farm that you passed earlier. Stay with the path along the woodland edge and where the pasture on the right ends swing left with the path back into the trees. In only a short distance you will come to a junction with a crossing track. Here you branch right and follow the track gently up, ignoring a track that soon comes in from the right, until you arrive at another T-junction with a crossing track.

Turn left now and follow the broad path as it continues to rise, ahead and above the trees you can see the rock outcrops on the Wrekin. In a while you again come to the woodland edge where to your right you can see the awful mass of the Power Station at Ironbridge. It is to be hoped, when it has concluded its useful life, that the planners will ensure its demolition and the restoration of the beautiful surrounds.

Continue with the gently rising track and ignoring a path going left stay with it as it follows the tree edge. Now follows an extremely pleasant stretch of slightly contoured walking along the south easterly base of the Wrekin. After some distance the track takes you down into a shallow gully, and then up the other side it swings slightly left to a knoll. In the pasture to your right you can see a bath that doubles as a water trough and way beyond that the disused quarries on Lawrence's Hill. A short descent with the track, to then swing right, will soon bring you to a point where the track meets a wire fence on the right and below which are the ruined remains of a brick building and a metal gate. Just a few yards ahead is the hairpin bend of an unmade road.

Turn left and up the unmade road towards the green corrugated outbuildings of Wrekin Cottage. Passing the cottage go over the gated stile to continue forward – ignoring the track on the right going downhill – to then swing left on the broader track that passes a large red warning sign indicating the firing range boundary. A line of these red warning signs, which advise you that it is safe to walk to the summit provided you keep them on your right, lead you past a tall metal flag pole – from which a red flag flies when firing is in progress – and then past the large radio mast. The ridge track you are now following is very broad and very much used so that the route through the hill fort ramparts could hardly be easier.

Inside the fort there is a triangulation pillar, at 1335 feet, and a toposcope. The fort is one of the many Shropshire sites reputed to have been the location for Caractacus' last stand against the Romans – though I prefer Caer Caradoc for that distinction.

On a clear day the views from the summit are quite spectacular and those immediately ahead to the South Shropshire hills are particularly so. Ahead and slightly below the summit are colourful, glazed rock outcrops – the evidence of volcanic activity.

After a suitable stop at the summit the walk continues in the same direction and commences its descent on a very clear path past the outcrops. The path follows the steeply descending ridge of the whale-back and keeps a steady direction. In a while the descent is interrupted by a track that crosses your path. Continuing forward your way now rises slightly for the short distance to Little Hill.

At the highest point of Little Hill there are two Scots Pine trees. Pass immediately left of them to again resume your descent on a clear path and following the same direction. Shortly your path goes over a crossing track, enters mature woodland, and then goes over another crossing track to reach a section where the path is slightly sunken – and usually muddy. Beyond this go over another crossing track and so descend gently down to the gate on the edge of the woods and so onto the surfaced Spout Lane again.

Turn right along the lane and follow it to a T-junction in front of 'The Hermitage'. Here go left – signed for Longwood and Eaton Constantine – and follow this lane to another T-junction where you turn right. Now follow this road to pass Longwood Farm and, opposite its entrance, the parish boundary stone dated July 1895. Arriving at another T-junction and a red Post Office letter box go left and then right along the lane signed for Dryton and Eyton on Severn. Follow this lane to the third field boundary on the left, which is about 600 yards along the lane, where there is a metal gate on the left and an oak tree on the right.

Go left through the gate and walk forward along the field edge to the corner opposite, keeping the hedge on your left. In the corner go through the gap into a second field and follow the same line still with the hedge on your left. Entering a third field your way is now forward on a field edge track, again with the hedge left, to finally reach a double metal gate onto the lane at Eaton Constantine.

Turn right along the lane and now walk back to your starting point.

Feet of Clay
Draycott Edge

If you have ever travelled the A515 between Lichfield and Sudbury – probably on your way to the Peak District – you cannot have missed the sudden descent of an unnamed escarpment into the delightfully dubbed village of Draycott in the Clay. The edge, running on a west/east line for over seven miles, is a quite outstanding feature of the surrounding landscape, dominating as it does the lowlands of the Dove Valley to the North. I shall call it Draycott Edge!

This circular walk takes in parts of the wooded escarpment, with its resident herd of deer, and couples it to the plain at its base. Much of the land in this area is in the ownership of the Duchy of Lanacaster.

DISTANCE: 9 miles
MAPS: Landranger (1:50,000) 128
Pathfinder (1:25,000) 851
PARKING: Woodedge Lane (GR 140291) just off the B5017 and 1¼ miles from the A515 at Draycott in the Clay *or* at the top of Buttermilk Hill (GR 109283)
PUBLIC TRANSPORT: Very limited service from Uttoxeter to Draycott in the Clay. Stevensons Service 402. From Draycott walk north-west along the B5017 to Woodedge Lane.
START/FINISH: Woodedge Lane (GR 140291)

ABOUT 100 yards on the left along Woodedge Lane – from its junction with the B5017 – there is a wide grassy verge with a stile in the hedge. Go over the stile and follow the left hand hedge to the field corner where you cross a fence stile and a stream. In the next field go forward with a hedge on your right and through a gap into another field where you now follow the left hedge to a wooden pole in the corner. Go through a gap in the corner and then cross the head of a narrow field – with a hedge on your right – to a fence stile. Cross this into a final field where you now swing half left to the far left corner where there is a stile leading onto the B5017.

At the road turn right and follow it for about 150 yards to meet a gate and step stile on the right. Cross the stile into a long sloping field and walk diagonally up it to the far right corner, aiming for a house right of

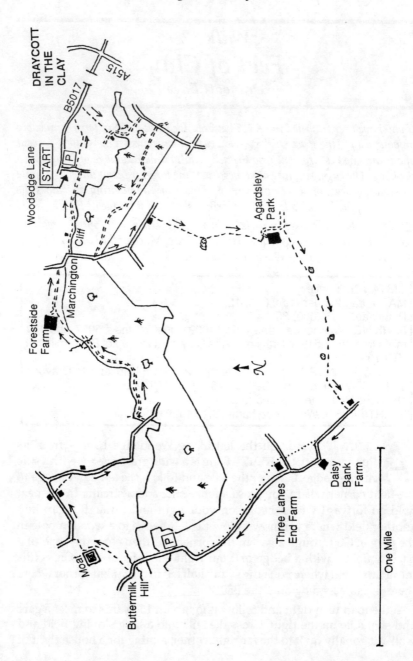

DRAYCOTT
IN THE
CLAY

A515

B5017

Woodedge Lane

START

P

Cliff

Marchington

Forestside
Farm

Agardsley
Park

N

Moat

P

Buttermilk
Hill

Three Lanes
End Farm

Daisy
Bank
Farm

One Mile

a white one. Arriving at a gate and stile in the corner – note the old water pump in the field – go over to join a narrow roughly surfaced lane on a bend in front of the house. Go directly forward (left) to pass 'The Old Nursery' – the white house. Just past 'The Old Nursery' the rough tarmac ends and the lane becomes a broad bridleway track as it ascends the Edge through woodland. Soon swinging left on a short section of embankment across a gully, the track continues to rise until meeting a metalled lane.

Here turn right and follow the lane for 175 yards when you will meet forestry roads coming in left and right. Take the right hand one and pass through its vehicle barrier to follow this broad, gravel, public bridleway along the ridge top. Shortly it swings left and then right to follow the edge of the woodland also. Some thinning of the trees has taken place which allows views across the vale below. Now continue following the forestry road for a further half mile to arrive at a house and a road.

Go left along the road and follow it to a junction where you stay with the major road, signed for Newborough and Burton. Continue for a further 300 yards from the junction to arrive at a cottage on the right. Immediately past the cottage and at the end of its garden go through a gate into a field. In the field go forward with initially the garden fence on your right and then the field hedge. Now walk the length of this long field to its corner where there is a fairly large pool. Go along the left edge of the pool for the few yards to the remains of a wooden gate mobilized as a fence. In front is a single strand barbed wire fence that is easily negotiated. Cross over it and go through the hedge gap at the side of the 'gate'.

In the next field your way is straight across, aiming for a gap in a protruding hedge corner. On arrival go through the gap and follow the now distinct track along the side of the left hand hedge towards Agardsley Park. Arriving in the field corner you will be faced with two gates. Pass through the left hand one to walk the few yards, left of a Scots Pine and other trees, to join the drive from the house. Go forward with the drive, keeping the farm and its buildings on your right, until immediately beyond the last of the farm buildings the farm drive swings sharp left. Here you go straight ahead into the corner where there is a cattle grid and a wooden signpost.

Crossing the cattle grid, turn right and follow the distinct tractor track – a bearing of 240 degrees – along the pasture to descend to another cattle grid and gate in a dip. Cross over and still following the track rise to pass immediately right of a pool. Here the track continues forward and then bends a little to meet a gate and stile in the hedge ahead. Cross the stile and walk upwards across the field, veering slightly right, towards a solitary tree in the distance and on a general bearing of 255 degrees. This will bring you to the pointed topmost right corner where at the very point there is a wooden step stile. Cross over immediately onto a farm track next to a gate and a pool.

From here cross the farm track (slightly right) and go across a field, effectively cutting the corner, heading for a barn in the far distance and right of a white house in the nearer distance – a bearing of 270 degrees, due west. Passing just left of a tree surrounded pool in the field you will come to a gateway in the hedge ahead. Go through and in the next field follow the same line heading for a point right of a tree that appears to be in the middle of the field. As you get nearer you will see that the tree is in fact in the hedge in front.

On reaching the hedge turn left to follow it into the bottom field corner. Here go left for 25 yards to a gate that you go through to pass a pool and reach a surfaced lane.

Now turn right along the lane to follow it past the white house and up through a left and a right bend – passing Daisy Bank Farm on the way – until reaching the lane junction at Three Lane Ends Farm. Take the lane directly ahead, left of the farm, and follow it for almost three quarters of a mile to a right bend.

NB. Both the OS and the Definitive maps show a tantalizing public footpath running alongside this lane – as well as one near Daisy Bank Farm – see the dotted lines on the sketch map. Regrettably, at the time of writing it was not negotiable so this quiet lane is described as an acceptable alternative. The matter has been reported to the County Council so, who knows?, the paths may have been opened up when you come to walk it!

At the right bend follow it round and then, ignoring the track right signed 'Duchy of Lancaster. Forest Banks', go left with another bend. Now follow the lane steeply down Buttermilk Hill. At the bottom cross the bridged stream and follow the lane for a further 65 yards up to a right bend where there is a step stile, gate and footpath sign on the right.

Cross over the stile and go forward to meet the left hedge which you follow forward to its protruding corner. Here leave the corner to go ahead and very slightly left to the right hand of a line of trees beyond which there is a church spire in the distance. As you near the trees you will see that they flank a square, water filled moat.

Though there is an absence of any historical record that positively identifies the origins of the moat, there is a reference in a survey of 1615 to a decayed manor house. It is believed that this 'lost' manor house was sited within the rectangle.

In the corner you will also see a stiled footbridge that you cross into another field to immediately turn left and follow the moat edge to another field corner. Here there is a step stile next to a wide gap in the hedge. Go over the stile – or through the gap – into the next field and turn right to follow the hedge into the bottom corner. At the corner go left for a few yards to a gate that you go through to then turn left in the next field to a stile in the corner near a gate. Cross the stile onto a surfaced lane.

Turning right follow the lane to reach the first cottage on the right, with its red painted outbuildings. Just past the cottage, and also on the right, is a gate into a field. Go through it and head down the field, slightly left, and aiming for a white house. Just above the bottom corner of the field there is a gate in the hedge on the left, go through it and join a lane. Here turn right to follow the lane over a stream and then start the climb up to the foot of Draycott Edge. In a while the lane swings left and then passes a T-junction and a farm. Still climbing, arrive at Cliff Cottage where the tree line and a public footpath sign is on the left.

Go left and follow the track initially along the side of Cliff Cottage. In a short distance you will meet another footpath sign with a waymarked stile on the left. Ignoring this continue forward with your track along the bottom of the Edge and just in the trees. In about half a mile, after passing more signs that merely indicate your way forward, you will come to a sign that points left to a hunter's gate. Go through it and turn immediately right to follow the fence, parallel to your previous track. In a few yards you will reach the field corner where you descend into a gully to cross a sleeper footbridge and on the other side a step stile. Go up the other side of the gully and continue to follow the fence and woodland edge. At a bend in the fence Forestside Farm comes into view. Continue forward and in a short distance a barbed wire fence leaves the woodland edge and heads for a blue metal gate to the right of the farm. Follow this fence and go through the gate to walk forward and join the farm road. Now follow the farm road forward, initially with a hedge on your right, until reaching the road at Marchington Cliff.

A right turn along and up the road will take you round a bend where, just after the second bend warning sign, a track with a red and green wooden post goes off left. Go left with the track, now with good views on your left, to pass a white house just beyond which your track is unsurfaced and soon becomes a hedged green lane. Follow the green lane to its end at a T-junction with a narrow surfaced lane – Woodedge Lane. Here just turn left back to your start.

Walk 13
A Sermon in Stones
The Roaches

A walk in a National Park, crags rising to 1547 feet, a woodland 'open air' church, a small resident band of wild wallabies – and all this in the county of Staffordshire!

Yes it's true. So what or where is this unique place? The 'what' is the Roaches, a Gritstone Edge stretching three dramatic miles. The 'where' is in North Staffordshire and just within the Peak District National Park.

This has to be one of my most favoured walks, so enough from me! Let's walk it and enjoy it.

DISTANCE: 10 miles
MAPS: Outdoor Leisure (1:25,000) 24
Landranger (1:50,000) 118 & 119
PARKING: Roadside Car Parking on unclassified road near Upper Hulme.
PUBLIC TRANSPORT: PMT Service X23 Hanley - Leek - Buxton. Alight on the A53 at the stop for Upper Hulme. Follow the unclassified road that twists through Upper Hulme and then heads north-west, north, then north-west again to the Roaches Car Park – a distance of 1½ miles.
START/FINISH: Car Park (GR 004621)

LEAVING the car parking area, which is little more than an elongated widening of the road near the drive to Pheasants Clough Farm, walk south to pass a small wooden sign on the right that pleads 'Please do not knock stones off this wall — Thank you', and in just a few yards reach a gate on the left. Go through the gate and immediately in front of you is a plaque giving information on the Roaches Estate, its acquisition and its wildlife management. Pass right of the plaque to follow a distinct track that rises gradually towards the pass between the Roaches left and Hen Cloud right.

Meeting a stone intake wall, keep it on your right and follow it until arriving at a step stile. Cross the stile and a pasture to the step stile opposite. Over this second stile you are now on open moorland again. Ahead of you is the distinct concessionary path up to the top of Hen Cloud from which good views of the surrounding countryside are

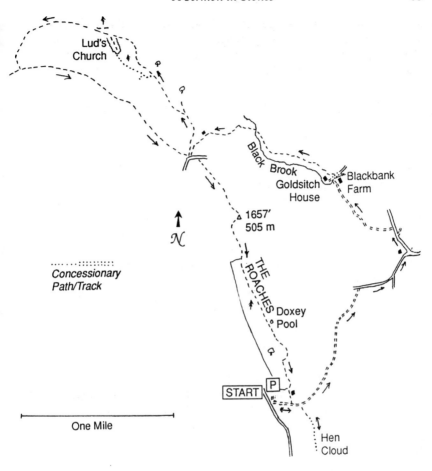

Lud's
Church

Black
Brook
Goldsitch
House

Blackbank
Farm

▲ 1657'
505 m

$\mathcal{N}$

Concessionary
Path/Track

THE ROACHES

Doxey
Pool

START

P

One Mile

Hen
Cloud

available — particularly Tittesworth Reservoir right and Ramshaw Rocks left.

Although it is possible to continue over the crest and then descend to a circling public footpath around the base of Hen Cloud, this public path can be a little indistinct in places and difficult in wet weather. In one particular spot there is also — in my view — a distinct hazard, so it is recommended that you retrace your steps from the summit of Hen Cloud, over the two stiles and so back onto your original track where you now go right.

Initially keeping the stone wall on your right, follow the track as it then veers left away from the wall, near another step stile. Stay with this grassy track that soon meets a wall and fence on the right and now follows them, rising gently. To your left is a ruined building and above it the serrated gritstone edges of the Roaches. Follow the track which in a while passes through a collapsed stone wall and then through a shallow gully. Your track is now more of a distinct path.

Arriving at an upright stone pillar, ahead of you are good views of the Staffordshire Moorlands. Soon the path meets the right hand wall and fence again to continue with them to a step stile leading into a fenced and unsurfaced farm road. Over the stile go left so as to follow the same line and then arrive at a gated stile that you cross to merge with another unsurfaced farm road coming in from the right. Continue following the same direction until, crossing a cattle grid, you join a metalled road.

Turn right along the road and follow it to pass another road coming in from the right and so continue up to a broad T-junction with yet another road. Here turn left, then after passing the sign and entrance for Newstone Farm on the right continue with the road for a further 70 yards where you will arrive at a step stile in the wall on the left. Cross the step stile and then immediately cross a footbridge over a boggy patch to walk forward with a fence and wall on your right — in the distance is the long ridge of the Roaches. Soon your path has the remains of a wall on each side and begins a gradual descent along the side of a small watercourse.

You are now on Goldsitch Moss, an area of peat moorland. Here, many years ago, small amounts of coal were mined for local consumption.

In a little while you will arrive at a fence corner where you now turn right — keeping the fence on your left — for just a few yards to a step stile that is waymarked with a yellow arrow and the message 'Follow fence line to farm'. Crossing the stile and keeping the fence on your left walk towards the farm, in a while crossing another stile at the side of a gate, and so arrive at the entrance to the farmyard of Blackbank Farm. Here a wooden footpath sign directs you through the farmyard and straight ahead between a wooden building left and farm buildings right. This line takes you over a cattle grid and then a bridged stream where you will meet another wooden fingerpost.

Here the Ordnance Survey map shows your right of way abruptly ending with no connection to the other right of way that crosses some 70 yards away. This anomaly might have prevented the walk you are embarked upon had not the National Park authorities negotiated a concessionary route to join the two rights of way.

The wooden finger post indicates the public footpath you have just followed with the usual yellow waymark arrow. The other finger of the post points right and is marked 'Concession Path' and bears a white arrow. Go right with the concession for the 70 yards or so along the farm road. On the right another wooden fingerpost now indicates the other

'Weather-sculpture' on the Roaches

public footpath that crosses left and right. On your left, immediately before this latter fingerpost, there is a stile next to a gate through which you cross. Now walk forward aiming for the right (and white) end of Goldsitch House ahead. This will bring you to the access track that you cross at the garden fence corner.

Keeping just right of an old bath doubling as a water trough, follow the edge of a very low embankment keeping well right of a fence at the side of Black Brook. Ahead of you is a gate in a stone wall that you now head for, crossing a wooden bridge on the way. Just before reaching the gate, to the left, you will see the remains of a stile where the wall ends near the brook. Cross this stile to swing left towards the fence next to the brook and so in a short distance reach a gate. Next to the gate is a stone squeeze stile that you go through to join the brook bank.

Now walk downstream with Black Brook left and a stone wall right. Keeping with the wall the path gradually rises above the stream (it's now getting too large to keep calling it a brook!) and crosses a small tributary watercourse just before a collapsed joining wall. Go through the gap of the collapsed wall — which is marked by the fallen stone pillars — and go forward now with the main wall on your left and the stream further left and below. In a short while a broken wall appears on your right so that you are following, at least for a short way, an enclosed path. In a short distance further the wall on your right disappears but your way forward is quite distinct with the remaining left wall. Now your path begins a descent back to the stream.

Back near the stream a gated step stile and a footpath sign awaits you. Cross the stile and walk the few yards to the metal footbridge ahead and so cross to the opposite bank. Now go directly forward with a wall on your right to follow a distinct path along the base of a hillside. After a while the path begins to rise and then swing left away from the wall. Stay with your path as it rises through the heather and arrives at the corner of a stone wall below a house. Continue forward with the wall on your right, soon passing left of the house to join its unsurfaced access road. Follow it upwards and forward to then pass another Roaches Estate sign on the right, next to a stepped squeeze stile. Do not cross this but continue with the access road to meet a surfaced moorland road at a bend.

Here you have a choice. If you wish to shorten the walk then continue from ➡ *(page 69); otherwise follow the directions in the next paragraph.*

At the edge of the surfaced road and to your right you will see a squeeze stile in the wall. Go through it and then immediately right over a wooden step stile so as to walk down the hill with the wall on your right. Soon passing the stepped squeeze stile you passed earlier — but on the other side — continue down the hill with the clear path and follow it as it swings left, away from the bottom corner of the wall, and heads towards woodland. Just before entering the mature woodland you cross a tiny stream and then just a few yards into the trees you will arrive at a wooden footpath sign amongst Scots Pine. Forward is signed for Gradbach whilst left is signed for Lud's Church. Go left with the path for Lud's Church that initially follows the woodland edge for some distance. Follow the clear path as it gradually gets a little deeper amongst the trees and then arrives at another wooden finger post at a junction of paths.

The right of way continues forward — yellow arrows and signed 'Swythamley' — whilst the path going left is a concessionary path signed with a white arrow for 'Lud's Church'.

While it is not necessary to follow the concessionary path to get to Lud's Church, nevertheless it is now described.

Turning left, follow the path for only a few yards where there is a wooden post on your left at another path junction. Do not take this left turn but continue forward to follow the concessionary path along the edge of the woodland. This will bring you to a wooden fence and a yellow waymark above Lud's Church. Go down the steps into the deep gully and walk between the steep sides of this cleft to emerge at the other end onto a crossing terraced path which is the right of way you left earlier.

To avoid the concessionary path and stay with the right of way; at the wooden finger-post you continue forward with the sign for 'Swythamley' and follow the clear path as it passes left of a fairly deep gully and proceeds through the woodland. After a while the path becomes more or less terraced and then comes to a cleft in the rocks on the left. It is easy to walk

Lud's Church

straight past this cleft so be on the look-out for it. At the entrance to the cleft is a stone inscribed 'Lud's Church'.

This deep tree topped cleft, which runs back some way into the hillside, is associated with much ancient mythology and on entering it is not difficult to understand why our superstitious ancestors' imagination ran riot! What is reasonably sure is that the site was used by the Lollards, one of the first groups of religious non-conformists in this country, who were fearfully persecuted during the fourteenth century. Mythology has it that Lud's Church is the Green Chapel of Sir Gawain's legendary battle with the Green Knight!

After making a detour to investigate Lud's Church return to the terraced right of way and continue walking in your original direction —

Rockhall Cottage

a roughly westerly course. In a short way you will meet a path coming in from the right, near a fingerpost and an outcrop of rocks. Continue forward on the merged path, again signed for Swythamley, and follow it as it swings left to arrive at the corner of a stone wall. Keeping the wall on your right stay with the path until it brings you to a gate and step stile with a wooden fingerpost. Do not cross the stile but instead turn left at the fingerpost to follow the path signed for Roach End.

Now begins an exhilarating ridge edge walk extending some three miles. While the walk up to now has been very good, you ain't seen nothing yet — the best has been saved till last! Route finding could not be simpler and now enables you to enjoy the superb views seen from the path.

Following the clear path as it rises, initially with a fence to the right, eventually you will cross a step stile and then carry on with a wall to your left. Arriving at a fence stile in the wall cross it and follow the same path along the edge where in a while it meets a wall coming in from the right and now follows it. Stay with this wall all the way to a gate and step stile, that you cross, and then go through a squeeze stile in the wall opposite to emerge onto the bend in the surfaced moorland road that you met earlier.

➡ Cross the road and take the made steps up the opposite side to initially follow the wall on the right. The broad track rises to pass between huge, marvellously shaped rocks that have weathered over the ages and then arrives at a triangulation pillar that stands at 1547 feet, the highest point.

Pass just left of the pillar and continue with the path as it follows the ridge edge and in a while passes between the edge right and Doxey Pool left. Doxey Pool is a typical shallow upland tarn, wild and frequently windswept.

It was here, some years ago, that I saw my first and only wild wallaby. If you are lucky enough to see one and then try telling your friends about it — be prepared for some strange looks! The Roaches are the main habitat for this small colony of war-time escapees from Swythamley Hall which, despite the odd severe winter and road accident, seem to have modestly thrived.

Beyond the pool your path begins its gradual descent — ahead in the distance you can see Hen Cloud — and in a while follows a wall on your right. Further on the path descends to the lowest part of a shallow saddle just before the end of the Roaches. Here the wall on your right ends, so turning right into a gully, descend stone steps to then swing left and walk between trees and the gritstone edge on your left.

Coming to the end of this lower shelf bear right with another stone wall and then sharply right down more stone steps to pass in front of the abandoned 'Rockhall' cottage to join the track below the enclosure wall. Just a few yards away is the track that you originally followed from the car park — join it and so complete an exhilarating walk.

Wallaby

Walk 14
The Edge of the World
Wenlock Edge

Wenlock Edge is one of those features that inspire awe and respect for the simple beauty that nature is so capable of providing. Running a total of 15 miles from the Ironbridge Gorge to Craven Arms its origins are in the Silurian period (420 million years ago) when it was formed from the accumulation of sediments and microbic life in the tropical sea that covered this area. The result is a unique escarpment of limestone, some 900 feet high and up to a mile wide, that provides a habitat for a distinctive range of flora and gives outstanding views across Shropshire.

With the option of three starting points, the walk takes in some 4 miles of this geological feature and also explores the pastoral beauty of the land below the edge. On a clear day you'll be glad you came!

DISTANCE: 11½ miles
MAPS: Landranger (1:50,000) 127 and 138
Pathfinder (1:25,000) 890, 910 and 911
PARKING: Car Park in Much Wenlock and two on Wenlock Edge at GR 614996 and 583976
PUBLIC TRANSPORT: Midland Red West Service 436/437 Shrewsbury - Bridgnorth. Alight at Much Wenlock
START/FINISH: Much Wenlock (GR 623997)

WE start this walk from Much Wenlock, a fascinating Shropshire market town with much of historic and architectural interest. Leaving the pay and display car park in Burgage Way go back to St. Mary's Road and turn right to follow it to the junction with the A458 next to a filling station. Here turn right and follow the main road as it swings left to pass the Gaskell Arms Hotel and the turn for the B4378. Further along the A458, and again on the left, you will see the remains of the town pound. Passing 'under' the dismantled railway bridge you will come to the junction with the B4371 – signed for Church Stretton – which you follow left as far as the Horse and Jockey pub.

Next to the pub is a narrow lane signed for Blakeway Hollow. Follow it to where the tarmac ends and then continue rising with it for a further 100 yards to where there is a waymark post on the right for Harley Bank

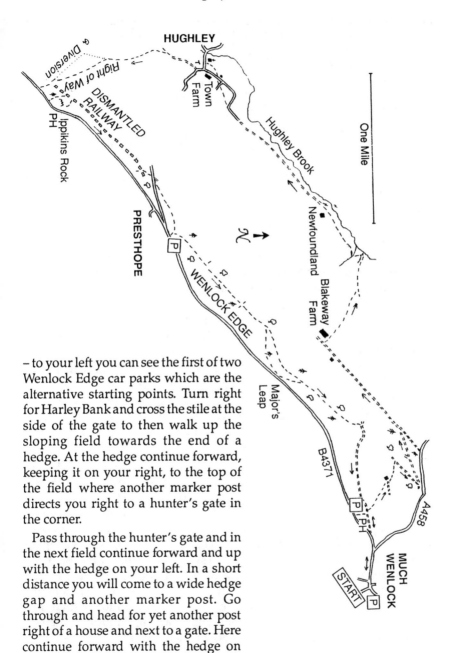

– to your left you can see the first of two Wenlock Edge car parks which are the alternative starting points. Turn right for Harley Bank and cross the stile at the side of the gate to then walk up the sloping field towards the end of a hedge. At the hedge continue forward, keeping it on your right, to the top of the field where another marker post directs you right to a hunter's gate in the corner.

Pass through the hunter's gate and in the next field continue forward and up with the hedge on your left. In a short distance you will come to a wide hedge gap and another marker post. Go through and head for yet another post right of a house and next to a gate. Here continue forward with the hedge on your left to a gate and hunter's gate at the corner of woodland. Through the gate follow the same line with the woodland fence on your right and so reach another hunter's gate in the top field corner. On the other side of the gate you now stand on the escarpment of Wenlock Edge itself.

At this point there is a waymark post indicating Blakeway Coppice to the left and Harley Bank right. Turn right to follow the escarpment edge as the path first descends steps and then rises again to soon become a wider track. Continue on this track, with good views through the trees to the left, until reaching a track T-junction and another marker post. Here go left, signed for Blakeway Coppice, and follow the track down the slope of the escarpment. At a fork take the right hand, lower branch and stay with this track to then join a hedged farm road at the bottom.

Go left along the unsurfaced farm road and follow it for almost a mile to pass Blakeway Cottage on the left and then arrive at a point immediately before the buildings of Blakeway Farm. On your left is a double gate and to your right a telegraph pole. The pole has a yellow waymark arrow pointing right to a gate behind it. Go through this gate and turn left – keeping the farm buildings and the hedge and fence on your left – to follow the edge of the field down to its bottom corner. In the corner there is a hunter's gate with a yellow (footpath) and a blue (bridleway) direction arrow. Pass through the gate and in the pasture follow the direction of the arrows forward to keep a line of trees on your right.

Reaching the fence at the bottom of the pasture – behind which there is a stream – swing left along the bottom of the field and so meet a tiny tributary stream. On the other side, and keeping the main stream to your right, continue forward gradually veering away from the main stream towards a second power pole and a scrubby bush. The bush houses a yellow waymark arrow that may not be too apparent at times of vegetation growth. However the arrow directs you slightly left of ahead and this line will soon bring you to a larger tributary stream and its crossing point. On the opposite bank is a step stile with waymark arrows.

This tributary stream is easily fordable, though gaiters might be an advantage after very heavy rain, so cross to the step stile and go over this. Now walk up the bank ahead to its brow above the trees fringing the main stream, Hughley Brook. Here swing left to follow the top of the bank, keeping Hughley Brook to your right and below, aiming for the right of a house, 'Newfoundland', in the distance. Arriving at a hedge corner right of 'Newfoundland' now join a farm road to continue forward passing to the right of the buildings. Passing through a gate you are joined by the house drive that now makes a good unsurfaced track across two large fields after which the track becomes a hedged green lane.

Passing another hedged green lane coming in from the left continue forward to a sharp right bend where in the left corner there is a gate and an ivy covered oak tree. At this point you will see from the sketch map that the right of way leaves the lane here to cut a corner and then join it again.

So, go through the gate and continue your same line – 250 degrees and aiming just right of the church spire – across the field to a stile in the boundary fence of a track. Cross the track to the opposite fence stile and enter a small field where you walk the short distance to the fence stile in the right hand hedge. This takes you back onto your original lane.

Opposite is a waymarked fence stile at the side of a gate. Cross over and go slightly left for the short distance to another waymarked fence stile. Over this go half left to the left corner of wooden stables which are themselves left of a bungalow. At the stable corner you will see a waymark arrow that takes you between the rear of the stables and the hedgerow to a corner step stile into a small field. Here follow the right hand fence to another step stile onto the tarmac lane in Hughley.

A few yards to the right along the lane is the very old church of St. John the Baptist with its unusual timbered tower and 'spire'.

From the church rejoin the lane and go left through the village. Passing a very old black and white timber framed house on the left you will arrive at a lane on the right with a telephone kiosk and letter box. Turn right here and follow the lane beyond the tarmac at the end of a row of cottages, to continue forward along the now unsurfaced lane. This soon empties into a narrow field where you continue forward with the right hand hedge and fence to its protruding corner where the field now opens out. Here go half left across the narrow neck to the protruding corner on the left from where you will see a waymarked step stile a short distance ahead. Over the step stile go slightly left across the next field to arrive at a gate in the hedge next to an oak tree. Go through the gate and half right with the direction of the arrow, across the field, aiming for the second of two protruding corners – a bearing of 170 degrees. At the protruding corner go forward with the field edge and stream to the inverted corner. Here turn left with the hedge and follow it for 40 yards to a metal gate.

Going through the gate walk straight across the narrow field to the gate opposite. Entering what appears to be a wide fenced track follow the left barbed wire fence as the enclosure opens out into a long narrow field. After about 200 yards you will come to a step stile in the left fence.

The Right of Way goes over this step stile into the field, to then go half right (155 degrees) across the field to a stile at the top right corner. However, at the time of writing there was what appears to be an unofficial diversion that simply continues along the narrow field, past the Right of Way, to a more substantial step stile in the farmost corner, next to woodland. The 'diversion' crosses this stile to follow the edge of the sloping field up to the stile in the top right corner where it rejoins the Right of Way.

Whichever way you follow cross over this top corner stile and, following the right hand hedge, walk the few yards up to the fence stile in the next corner which gives access into the woodland on the flank of Wenlock Edge. Entering the woodland your way ahead is straight up the embankment along a cleared path through the trees when you will soon reach the dismantled railway line – Craven Arms to Ironbridge.

Here you have a choice. If you wish to visit the Wenlock Edge Inn then follow the directions in the next paragraph. If not, then turn left along the railway line and follow the directions from ➡ below.

For the pub go straight across to follow the direction of the marker post opposite to continue forward and up. Shortly reaching a cross track go right with it for 50 yards when you will see another marker post indicating a left turn up the embankment again. So turn left here and follow the cleared path up to a hedge gap and a public footpath sign at the B4371. Turn left along the road and in 100 yards pass another public footpath sign on the left – remember this for later. From here you will see the Wenlock Edge Inn further along the road – this is your objective!

Leaving the inn retrace your steps along the B4371 for 250 yards to the footpath sign you noted earlier. Go right with it to follow the woodland path down the edge, going over the cross track encountered earlier, and so on down to meet the railway bed where you turn right.

➡ In a short while you will come to a marker post on the right indicating Ippikins Rock. Although this is a slight detour it is well worth the effort as the rock provides a superb viewpoint across the county to the Shropshire Hills.

So, turning right at the post, walk up the wide track until soon reaching another marker post directing you right, up a step, and onto a path. Follow the graded path through the trees, passing below a rock face, to soon reach the stile onto Ippikins Rock. Here legend tells of a bandit trapped in his cave by a falling rock! Having taken in the views just retrace your steps back to the railway bed where you now turn right.

In just under a mile you will come to another marker post for Ippikins Rock on the right and on the left a hunter's gate and a step stile. Go left over the stile and follow the track down to meet the Hughley road. At the road go right and up for the 35 yards necessary to meet the pole barrier and footpath marker on the left indicating Presthope. Go through the barrier and follow the cleared footpath through the trees until reaching steps that you descend into a sunken cross track. Here another marker post indicates right 'Presthope ¼ m'. Turn right and follow the sunken track up the edge to ascend wooden steps near the top. You then join a track on a bend just before the gate into a second Wenlock Edge car park – your other alternative starting point. Do not go through the gate but on the bend go left – with the red arrow for Blakeway Coppice – and follow the broad track down to a junction. Here continue forward – signed for 'Much Wenlock 3 m' – and stay with this track for about a mile when you will meet a marker post indicating a bridleway going right, up steps, to Major's Leap.

Legend has it that this is the spot where Major Smallman, of nearby Wilderhope Manor, leapt from a crag in his successful escape from Parliamentary pursuers during the Civil War. I am assured there is no connection with Prime Minister John Major! If you make this detour do note that the track continues from Major's Leap to the end of the huge quarry to then rejoin the main track 1¼ miles further along just before a wooden gate. There is no need to retrace your steps.

If you don't make the detour then simply stay with the main track, ignoring side tracks, to pass two bench seats and arrive at another junction where you take the right upper fork. In a while a signed path from Major's Leap rejoins your track and at this point Much Wenlock is three quarters of a mile away. Stay with your main track to soon arrive at a wooden gate across it. On the other side of the gate walk the few yards forward to a T-junction of tracks and another marker post. Left is signed for Harley Bank but you go right along the hedged green lane and follow it for about three quarters of a mile, all the way back to the Horse and Jockey pub on the B4371. From there make your way back to Much Wenlock.

Jay

Walk 15
The Hanchurch Hills
Meaford

Many's the time I've travelled north along the M6 motorway between junctions 14 and 15 and been intrigued by the tree clad slopes on the left. After all those years I finally managed to get there and explore. This walk is the surprising result.

Starting and ending near Meaford, an obvious and ancient crossroads, not only does this circular route take in the Hanchurch Hills but it also passes through an estate village with twin churches, follows ancient trackways and extensive woodlands to finally pass three historic archeological sites. Another feature of this walk is the abundance of rhododendron bushes.

DISTANCE: 12 miles
MAPS: Landranger (1:50,000) 127
Pathfinder (1:25,000) 830
PARKING: Lay-by on A51 or Hanchurch Hills car park and picnic area (GR 839397)
PUBLIC TRANSPORT: PMT Service X60/X260 Stafford - Stoke-on-Trent. Alight at junction with A51 and walk carefully north-west, then west along the A51 for about a mile to reach the farm road on your left. Then continue reading from the second paragraph below.
START/FINISH: Lay-by on A51, one mile west of Meaford (GR 871359)

FROM the lay-by walk eastwards along the A51 passing a gate on the right giving access to greenhouses, to then pass a covered reservoir on the left. Just beyond the reservoir, and on the right, you will quickly come to a farm road. Turn right to follow this hedged road and soon you will see the M6 motorway ahead and a bridge crossing it.

Follow the farm road to the bridge and on the other side of the motorway continue forward through Blakelow Farm keeping the white farmhouse on your left and old stables on your right. Continue forward on the farm track, now with a hedge on your left. At a bend, with a pool on the right, swing left and right with the track to now follow a hedge on the right. Arriving at a cattle grid cross it to turn right along the narrow surfaced lane.

This lane passes through Swynnerton Park and as such is very quiet. Following it for almost a mile will take you past the estate buildings, the Hall, the two churches and then to the road through the village. Turn right along the road towards the Fitzherbert Arms and immediately before the pub turn left along Early Lane. Follow the lane past the village hall to the last houses and the end of the tarmac. Now continue straight ahead into a hedged track and follow it for some way until it enters a large field at a wooden footpath sign.

Here the right of way follows a straight line to the A519 but, to avoid a large field crossing, a concessionary route has been arranged and signposted – see sketch map. This is now described.

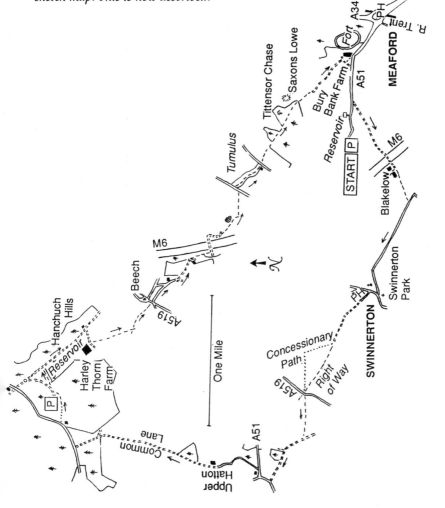

The wooden footpath sign indicates 'Hanchurch Walk' straight ahead so walk forward to follow the field edge on a broad track and with the hedge on your right. At the next field corner pass through the hedge gap where there is another wooden finger post. This indicates left so go with it to follow the edge of this second field now with a hedge on your left. This line will bring you to a public footpath sign on the A519.

Directly across the road is another footpath sign for 'Hanchurch Walk'. Cross to it and then go through the metal gate to follow a path along a field edge with a hedge and fence on your left. In a while this path will bring you to a field corner where there is a hunter's gate and a white wicket gate left of a cottage. Go through the gate onto a hedged and fenced green lane to turn right and pass the cottage. Continue with the green lane and follow it as it swings left and down to meet a road. Turn right and follow the road to a T-junction with the A51. Opposite are the elegant buildings and chimney stack of Hatton Pumping Station.

Turn right along the A51 and in a few yards left along the signed No Through Road at the side of the pumping station. Arriving at a corner – ahead is a no entry sign – go left with the bend in the road and then rising follow a bend right to pass a farm. Continue forward through a gateway and soon through another to follow the broad track, which is now unsurfaced, into a small valley. Your unsurfaced track is in fact named Common Lane on the Pathfinder O.S. map and you now follow it for over a mile as it becomes a broad, sandy and delightful walk up to the tree clad Hanchurch Hills.

At the end of Common Lane you will meet a gate giving access onto a tarmac road. Join the road and go right to follow it to 'Keepers Cottage' – a detatched house. Immediately past the house, at a bend in the road, there is a wooden kissing gate and Hanchurch Walk sign in the right corner.

This next section to the car park and picnic area is a concessionary path. The land in the vicinity of the covered reservoir was given to the County by Lord Stafford in 1960

Go through the kissing gate and take the left of two tracks (signed) up through the trees to another kissing gate. Through this go half left across the picnic area to the car park and gravel access road which you follow right to pass left of a brick tower. At the corner of the iron fence around the reservoir go right to follow it to the next corner. Here turn right to follow the perimeter fence and pass a derelict Water Board house. To your left and through the trees is the Hanchurch Hills escarpment.

Following this broad track for almost half a mile you will come to a T-junction of tracks with a pair of semi-detached cottages to the left. Turn right with the Hanchurch Walk sign and, ignoring the drive immediately right for Harley Thorn House, go through the gateway and along the road for Harley Thorn Farm. Along the farm road, just beyond a white gate on the right and immediately in front of a large house, there is a metal signpost. Forward is signed for the Hanchurch Walk, while to the left the sign indicates a public footpath. Turn left at this signpost and go over the step stile next to the right hand of two adjacent gates and so into a field. Walk forward with the fence and hedge on your left, to the right are fine views across the Staffordshire countryside. Where the hedge swings left towards the field corner you go straight on to the gate and step stile a few yards ahead in the opposite hedge.

In the next field continue the same line across the field and so arrive at a gated step stile into a broad, grassy, hedged and fenced track. Cross the stile into the track and go to the stile immediately on your left. Cross into a field and walk slightly right (initially a bearing of 110 degrees) across the centre of the field. When you can see the opposite hedge, start to go a little more right to a broad hedge gap and public footpath sign onto the A519 near a telephone kiosk.

Cross the main road and take the little lane opposite. Follow it to pass a joining lane left and then beyond the No Through Road sign pass a farmhouse also on the left. Soon arriving at 'The Old Cottage' you are immediately faced with a parting of the ways. Take the left fork to pass right of a pool and then a timber framed house with a large ruined caravan. Continue forward through a gateway and into the hedged and fenced track which has a sign saying 'Road to Farm Only' but also has a sign stating 'Public Footpath Winghouse Lane'. Follow the track as it proceeds to the entrance into the farmyard. Before the entrance, and attached to the corner of an old brick building on the left, is a large footpath sign that points left. Go left with the sign and follow the clear path through trees, left of the farm buildings, on the edge of an escarpment. Immediately below you is the M6 motorway.

Walking parallel with the motorway the path now gradually descends to reach a step stile on the edge of the trees. Cross it to continue down the bank to the right hand of two oak trees on the edge of the cultivated part of the field. Walking directly across the field aim for the end of the wooden fencing ahead. On arrival you will see a step stile on the left giving access into a fenced track. Go over it and forward to cross the motorway bridge. On the other side follow it right along the side of the motorway. As it then swings left you will immediately see the remains of a gate in front of you and a notice on the right hand fence stating 'Highway Code Ruling. Keep to footpaths at all times. When cattle or sheep are in this field dogs must be kept on a lead.'

Cross the fence at this sign and go half left – a bearing of 130 degrees – across the field. In a short way you will see a pool ahead. Walking closely to the right of it you then pass between two clumps of gorse and so reach a step stile a short distance in front. Over this stile turn immediately right over a sleeper footbridge and follow the bottom edge of the next field with a barbed wire fence on your left. In about 50 yards you will come to a sleeper footbridge on the left with a step stile on the other side. Cross both into a sloping field and walk up with the hedge on your left to the top corner where steps take you up to a stile and so onto a road.

Turn left along the road for a little less than 50 yards where on the right there is a gate gap and a public footpath sign for Chase Lane. *Now you start the last two miles that contain no less than three antiquities. Very little is known of these as investigations have only recently commenced.*

Go through the gate gap and follow the clear path through the thin strip of trees, on your left is the mound of a prehistoric tumulus. Carry on with the fenced area as it narrows and tends right to arrive at a surfaced lane left of a large house. Cross the lane to the public footpath sign opposite and go over the step stile at the side of the gate. Continue forward for a short way to cross another step stile, right of two adjacent gates, and so enter a fenced path. Walk forward, crossing another step stile, and up to follow the broad clear path as it enters the woodland. You are now on Tittensor Chase with good views left through the trees and many rhododendrons lining the path. Keeping straight ahead along this delightful path, and with the single strand wire fence on your right, you will eventually come to the end of the woodland with a gate left and a gate right, both with barbed wire along the top.

Pause here to view Saxons Lowe on the left – a burial mound – that has obvious connections with Bury Bank Hill Fort not too far ahead.

From this point walk the few yards forward along the fenced path to a stile into a field. Cross the centre of the field aiming for the wooden electricity pole ahead. Before it passes the pole the path becomes a broad track. It then passes a small pool on the right to pass through a hedge gap now with a hedge on the left. Stay with the track as it continues forward and then changes to the other side of the hedge near an electricity pylon. Follow it as it now rises to a T-junction in front of Bury Bank Farm. To your left is the tree clad hill fort (Bury Bank Hill Fort).

At the T-junction go right for about 50 yards to a step stile in the fence on the left. Cross it to follow the garden fence on the left and so reach a stile by a footpath sign onto the A51. Now turn right to follow the broad verge of the A51 back to the lay-by (or, if using public transport, turn left to return to the bus stop on the A34).

Walk 16
Hallowed Places
Worcester

Not many rural walks start in a city centre but this one does – in Worcester. As well as a pleasing landscape the walk takes in the ever popular River Severn, Elgar's birthplace and museum, the ancient Powick Bridge, the first large scale hydro-electric plant in the world, the River Teme, the site of the last battle of the Civil War – and the start of Charles II's flight to France – plus the many attractions of Worcester itself not least being the Cathedral and the Commandery.

DISTANCE: 12½ miles
MAPS: Landranger (1:50,000) 150
Pathfinder (1:25,000) 996
PARKING: Public Car Parks in Worcester
PUBLIC TRANSPORT: Numerous bus services or British Rail to Worcester
START/FINISH: Worcester Bridge (GR 847548)

CROSS Worcester Bridge to the west bank of the River Severn and turn right along Henwick Parade to now follow the riverside path. Walk under the railway bridge as it crosses the river and in a while pass Worcester Racecourse on the opposite bank. After quite some time following the river, and passing some very large houses on the other bank, you will see left and slightly ahead beyond the power lines the spire of Hallow church. Before drawing level with it you will arrive at a signpost which is also the city boundary and which indicates ahead along the river, 'Hallow ¾ mile' and 'Bevere Lock 1 mile'. Signed to the left is 'Hallow Road'. Stay with the river to pass under the power lines as they cross to the opposite bank. Continue on the riverside path to a point where, on the left, you are level with Hallow church and the tall white chimneys of Hallow Park. Here your river path crosses a stile into a field and here you leave the river.

Having crossed the stile and its footbridge turn left and follow the left hand fence. Passing a gate on the left continue forward to a step stile and cross it into a field at the bottom of a slope below the white chimneys. Go forward and up the bank to meet a cross track rising from left to right.

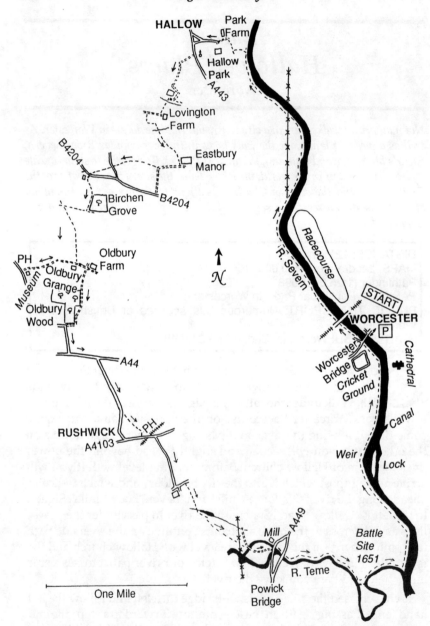

Worcester. The Severn in flood

Turn right along the grassy track and walk to a gate and stile before Park Farm. Over the stile go immediately left, parallel with another track, to follow a wire fence on the left. This brings you to a minor tarmac road (Church Lane) by a graveyard. Follow it to pass left of Hallow village green and so join the A443.

Go left along the main road to reach the gateway into the churchyard immediately before the church itself. On the opposite side of the road is a tarmac lane with a public footpath sign. Turn right with the sign and follow the lane that very quickly opens out to a hedge on the right and an open field on the left. Continue forward, still following the tarmac as it follows the field boundary and swings left above an escarpment. Stay with the tarmac around the edge of the field and in a while follow it as it again swings sharp left. Below on the right is a water treatment plant. Go forward to then skirt the plant by going right and right again to reach double metal gates topped with barbed wire.

Down and to your left is a broad footbridge over a stream. Cross it and go through a metal hunter's gate to walk up the sloping field with a fence and hedge on your left. At the protruding hedge corner leave it to cut the field corner and pass immediately right of Lovington Farm through a wooden hunter's gate and onto the farm drive at two gates.

On the farm drive go right and pass under power lines to a point where the drive becomes hedged on both sides. Here there is a step stile and footpath sign in the left hand fence that you go over to follow a fenced path. Go forward then left and right as the path descends into a shallow valley and crosses a little stream. On the other bank walk straight across the centre of the sloping field aiming for a large tree at the top of the rise on a bearing of 150 degrees. Immediately before the tree you will arrive at a protruding hedge corner.

Ahead is Eastbury Manor. Pass through the gateway in the hedge corner, continuing forward with a fence on your left, to pass right of the Manor and exit the field through a gate in the corner onto a tarmac drive. Turn right along the drive which is also a bridleway – look for the bunches of mistletoe in the large tree – and where the tarmac makes a sharp left turn you go straight ahead through a gateway, near a bridleway sign, and so into a field.

In the field go forward with a hedge on your right until it disappears. Continue forward across the large gap to the point where the hedge re-appears. Here still continue forward on the same line but this time keep the hedge on your left. In the field corner go through a wooden hunter's gate onto a metalled lane. Opposite is a black metal gate that you go through to follow the left hand hedge of the field to reach another black metal gate immediately left of a white cottage. Go through the gate and so join the B4204.

Cross over the road and take the farm track directly opposite at the side of Sandbank Cottage – ignore the footpath sign a few yards right along the B4204. Immediately before the gate at derelict farm buildings there is a rotten stile on the left where the footpath is totally overgrown. This leaves little alternative but to go through the gate and immediately left in front of the derelict buildings to pick up the line of the path in the field corner – a matter of a few yards. Here go forward with the fence and hedge on your left heading for the right of Birchen Grove. At the end of the grove and in the field corner there is a fence stile that you cross into a large field. Turn immediately right and follow the top edge of the field with the hedge and fence on your right. To the left are grand views of the Malvern Hills.

In about 300 yards you will come to a wooden step stile in the hedge. Here you go left across the field – slightly back on yourself – to follow a bearing of 160 degrees that heads for the lower part of the field boundary below Oldbury Grange. Following this line will bring you to a step stile and footbridge in the hedge next to a tree. On the other side your line is now up the slope on a bearing of due south. This brings you to a wooden step stile immediately behind a double wooden electricity pole slightly left of Oldbury Grange.

Crossing the stile join an unsurfaced lane. If you wish to visit Elgar's birthplace museum and the nearby pub then follow the directions below, if not then go left on the unsurfaced lane and through the hunter's gate between the two gates in front. Now read from ➡ below.

Turn right to follow the unsurfaced lane for just under half a mile to the road at Broadheath, next to Elgar's birthplace and museum. The pub is along the road to the right.

From the museum retrace your steps along the unsurfaced lane to the point in front of Oldbury Grange where you crossed the stile earlier but this time go forward and through the hunter's gate between the two gates in front of you.

➡ Joining the drive from Oldbury Grange continue forward and where the tarmac swings right go through the hunter's gate ahead at the side of a larger gate. You are now on a junction of tracks near the farm. Go right through a gate – in a few yards passing the drive to Oldbury Grange! – to follow the roughly surfaced hedged and fenced lane towards Oldbury Wood. Stay with the lane as it passes the wood and finally swings right to meet a road on a bend. Turn left along the road and follow it to the T-junction with the A44.

Powick Mills and Old Powick Bridge

New Powick Bridge

Go left on the pavement along the A44 to reach Claphill Lane on the right. Turn right into Claphill Lane, which is signed for Rushwick, and follow it for about half a mile – ignoring the first public footpath signs left and right – to reach a bend in the lane and, on the left, October Cottage. Immediately after October Cottage, also on the left, is a public footpath sign for Bransford Road that you follow to enter a field. In the field go right, keeping a hedge on your right, to follow it down to a corner behind 'The Whitehall' pub. Go through the gate on the right next to the pub and join the A4103.

Turn left along the A4103 and over the railway bridge to turn right along Upper Wick Lane which is a signed 'No Through Road'. Immediately pass a footpath sign on the right and stay with Upper Wick Lane for a little under half a mile until reaching a crossroads in front of Upper Wick Farm and its letter box. Go left and follow the lane for 100 yards where, on the right, there is a footpath sign for Powick Hams together with a fence stile and a gate.

Cross the stile to enter an orchard and follow the right hand fence to its protruding corner. At the corner leave the fence and continue forward between the line of trees to follow the fairly clear path down to a stiled footbridge. This is a popular spot for herons. Cross the footbridge and head for the fence stile at the corner of woodland.

Over this stile follow the woodland edge on your left for approximately 80 yards where the right of way strikes forward across the field on a bearing of 130 degrees to pass through a gate into a second field and so forward to pass under power lines and arrive at a substantial bridge over a broad mill race.

On the other side of the bridge continue forward to a gate and bar stile into a hedged green lane which you follow to the old Powick Bridge and Mill with its brick chimney stack.

Here is an excellent example of the use of water power, in fact the mill was formerly the City of Worcester electricity works – the first large scale hydro-electric power station in the world.

Go left on the bridge and then swing right opposite the chimney stack to follow the signposted riverside path along the banks of the River Teme. Soon pass under the A449 road bridge and now follow the river as it meanders on its way to the River Severn. Crossing over riverside stiles you will arrive at one with a red painted post and on the other side the number 8. Over it continue with the bank for a short way to meet a barbed wire fence near a post with the number 7. Here the Teme makes a large loop and this is the narrowest part of the neck. Simply turn left with the fence and, ignoring the gateway and following the red splash and arrow, again pick up the bank of the Teme – a mere 40 yards. Now just continue to follow the Teme to its confluence with the Severn.

In 1651 the fields to your left were the scene of the Battle of Worcester. This was the end of Charles II's hopes of regaining the crown by force of arms and was also the start of his many trials and tribulations in effecting his escape to France.

Arriving on the bank of the River Severn simply turn left to follow this mighty waterway all the way to Worcester Bridge and the city. On the way you will pass a lock, a weir, a canal junction and, those two hallowed places – the cathedral and the county cricket ground! At Worcester Bridge just turn right to arrive back in the city.

Lapwing (Peewit)

Walk 17
Tinker, Tailor
Highgate Common

Highgate Common is a Country Park created by Staffordshire County Council consisting of 300 acres of birch woodland and heath. With good access and parking it makes a convenient start for this circular walk that follows an interesting route, not too far from the conurbation, taking in quiet villages and two smaller ridgeways. In part it links with the Staffordshire Way, the Long Distance Footpath that runs from the Cheshire boundary in the north to the Hereford and Worcester boundary in the south.

On a hot summer's day you will be accompanied by the gentle drone of light aircraft from the nearby Halfpenny Green Airport.

By starting and finishing at New Lodge Car Park you can shorten the walk by almost three miles if you so wish.

Distance: 12½ or 10 miles
MAPS: Landranger (1:50,000) 138 & 139
Pathfinder (1:25,000) 912 & 933
PARKING: Majors Car Park plus many others on Highgate Common
PUBLIC TRANSPORT: Midland Red West Service 585/586/587 from Wolverhampton to Trysull. Join walk at point marked ➤ on page 92.
START/FINISH: Majors Car Park, Highgate Common (GR 835897)

A T Majors Car Park face the road entrance and to your right you will see a horizontal, wooden vehicle barrier. Go through it to follow the track forward and then in a little while right to keep the woodland edge fence on your left. Staying with the woodland fence and passing another parking area – New Car Park – this track will narrow and bring you to a metalled minor road. Directly opposite is a track with another horizontal vehicle barrier across it. Cross the road and go through the barrier to follow the track down to a gate near a Staffordshire Way sign left and a blue topped bridleway marker post right.

From here to the New Lodge Car Park you will be following a bridleway that is waymarked by blue topped wooden posts with a white horseshoe superimposed. This bridleway is also the Staffordshire Way which is also waymarked

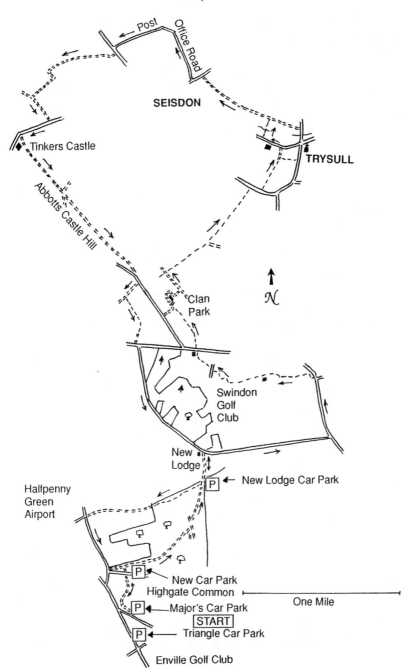

Post Office Road

SEISDON

Tinkers Castle

TRYSULL

Abbotts Castle Hill

Clan Park

Swindon Golf Club

New Lodge

New Lodge Car Park

Halfpenny Green Airport

New Car Park
Highgate Common

One Mile

Major's Car Park

START
Triangle Car Park

Enville Golf Club

N

with the Staffordshire Knot symbol. As a result, finding your way to the New Lodge Car Park should present no difficulties whatsoever. Nonetheless the route is now described.

So, turning right, follow the marker post and in a short way at a junction in the path bear right with the blue Staffordshire Knot arrows to join another track. Here go left with the new track and stay with this bridleway to follow it through pleasant mixed woodland. As one might expect in a Country Park there are many side tracks and paths but ignore them until arriving at a crossing bridleway with its own blue marker posts. Go left with it for the short distance to a Staffordshire Way sign where you turn right to continue your original line on the bridleway. In a while, approaching the edge of the common, your way swings left and in a short while right again to continue forward to a vehicle barrier pole and so onto the sandy New Lodge Car Park.

Here go straight ahead with the direction of the Staffordshire Way sign to follow a broad track to the tarmac road at New Lodge. Turn right along this quiet road – to the left is Swindon golf course – and follow it for about three-quarters of a mile to a T-junction. Go left to follow the road through Smestow where, after half a mile and on the left, you will arrive at a signed public footpath and step stile opposite Smestow Lane and just before a left bend in the road.

Cross over the stile and turn immediately right into the field corner where there is another footpath sign now pointing left. Turn left and keeping the hedge on your right follow it to the far field corner where a step stile awaits you. In the next field turn directly right into the corner where again you go left to follow the field hedge towards buildings. Passing between the brick building and the hedge swing left and right to continue following the hedge to the field corner. Here there is another step stile and footpath sign directing you onto the Swindon golf course.

On the other side go up the flight of wooden steps ahead. Now you follow a zigzag, but waymarked, route across the golf course.

At the top of the steps a yellow waymark arrow points you right. Follow it to the top hole – No. 3, but remember hole numbers can change! – where you now go left to pass between a waymark arrow and a sign stating 'Hole 4 – 120 yards – Stroke 2'. Arriving at another arrow on the right before the fourth green follow it right between saplings and cross in front of the fifth hole. Continue forward, on the left is a sign 'Hole 6 – 145 yards – Stroke 5', and soon arrive at a waymark arrow on the right and pointing right. Follow it through a gap in the trees soon emerging to see a white brick building to your left.

Walk to the building and the vehicle barrier right of it where there is a waymark arrow. Crossing the club road and following the direction of the arrow keep just left of the black and white aiming pole to head for the woodland where there is a gap and a track taking you through the silver birches. Soon arriving at another grass area go straight across heading for the house seen through the trees. Pass through the thin band of trees to the garden fence where you bear right to now pass right of the house and through a gate onto the road.

Cross directly over the road to the footpath sign and gate opposite. Go through the gate and forward on a fairly broad track with a hedge on your left. Leaving this area at the corner enter a field. Ahead in the field you will see a line of telegraph poles, the first of which bears a waymark arrow. Go to it and then follow the remainder of the poles to a wide gap in a hedge just before a bend in the drive to Clan Park Farm.

Here go directly forward with the drive and where the drive branches right into the farmyard you continue ahead to pass left of the buildings and then bear right between a pool and the rear of the farmhouse. Stay with the farm track to swing left when the track soon meets a crossing green lane. Leave the farm track here and turn left into the green lane to follow it for just over 200 yards as far as a large gap on the right where tractors enter a field. A footpath crosses the green lane at this point and the lane narrows appreciably. Another identifier is a large tree stump in the gap.

Turn right through the gap and follow the edge of the field with the hedge on your right. This will bring you to another gap in the next corner. Go through it and in the next field walk straight across heading for a point immediately left of a large holly bush that you can see ahead – a bearing of 60 degrees.

As you approach the holly bush you will be able to see a gap left of it. Go through the gap and across the next field aiming well left of a solitary tree in the furthest right corner, this is now a bearing of 40 degrees. In fact the point you are aiming for is the left edge of the remaining hedge (from the tree) and as you get there you will see that at some time in the dim distant past it was a gateway. Now, in the fifth and last field, go straight across, aiming for the large white house in the distance that is itself left of greenhouses. This line will bring you to a stile in the opposite hedge giving access onto a lane.

Go right along the lane for about 100 yards to a point where there is a hedge gap right and double gates left. Pass left through the gates and cross the concrete base to follow a broad track across the field towards the right hand of the greenhouses mentioned earlier. Passing the greenhouses the track goes through a gateway with a hedge on the right and a wall on the left. Soon arrive at two gates in close proximity both with step stiles at the side. Go over both and forward between farm buildings to a road and turn left along this.

▶ *If you are starting from Trysull begin here.*

Pass the Manor House, then the speed derestriction signs and then, just after the Trysull sign, arrive at double gates on the right set back off the road. The right hand gate is signed 'Aintree' and the left one 'Ascot'! Go over the step stile at the side of the left hand 'Ascot' gate and then forward onto the sleeper bridge over the Smestow Brook. Just ahead is a second bridge that you cross to follow the right edge of the field up a bank to a protruding corner. Here go forward, across the field, to a step stile and signpost in the opposite hedge.

Cross the stile into a green lane and go left to follow it for a little over half a mile to a surfaced road on the edge of Seisdon. Turn left along the road and then right into Post Office Road.

Now following Post Office Road continue with it for about three-quarters of a mile until it meets a T-junction with another road. Here go left and immediately right into a track displaying the Staffordshire Way blue arrow. Follow it as it swings right past an electricity sub station. Hedged on both sides it gently rises to pass left of huge farm buildings to continue as a hedged track to a Staffordshire Way sign and a hunter's gate right of a green corrugated metal building. Go through the hunter's gate and follow the hedged and fenced bridleway forward to a corner where it goes left and then right to continue up and meet a surfaced farm road. Go left along the farm road – you are now just below Wolmore Ridge – until meeting a road. Here turn right and follow the road to the top of Tinkers Castle Hill where there is a large white crenellated house.

Immediately before the house and on the left there is a fenced bridleway. Follow it as it progresses along the edge of the garden and so onto Abbots Castle Hill proper. Now follows a mile of good ridge walking through mixed woodland and with views on the right across Shropshire. For a short distance you are actually on the county boundary.

Follow your bridleway along the ridge ignoring side tracks and keeping to the highest point with fields left and the tree covered edge right. After some distance the way broadens and then descends to meet the B4176. Joining the road cross over to the track opposite that is marked with Staffordshire Way public footpath sign. Follow the track to a point where overhead power lines cross it and where there is a broad gap in the left hedge. Go left through the gap to follow a field edge – make sure it is the right one, the hedge should be on your left! Now follow the grassy track to the next corner where you go through a gap by a signpost. Follow the path between the hedge left and an embankment right that hides a sand quarry. Shortly the path swings right to arrive alongside the gate into the quarry. Joining the unsurfaced road from the quarry walk up to a metalled road.

Now turn left and then immediately right along the lane almost opposite. Follow it for a little over half a mile, passing on the way greenhouses and two houses, to New Lodge that you passed on your outward journey. At New Lodge turn right and follow the track to New Lodge Car Park.

Here you have a choice. Straight ahead with the Staffordshire Way sign will enable you to retrace your steps back to the start. But for a different way read on.

At the car park circle go to the other bridleway on the right, signed with the now familiar blue topped posts. Your clear bridle-path follows the woodland edge, just inside the trees, with fields to the right. At the end of the woodland it enters a hedged green lane and further on passes houses to join the road where opposite is Halfpenny Green Airport.

Turn left along the road and follow it for just over a quarter of a mile where, immediately before a T-junction left signed for Swindon and Himley, there is a Staffordshire Way marked bridleway also on the left. Entering the fenced bridleway follow it to another Staffordshire Way signpost next to the gate you met shortly after commencing your walk. Here go right up the track and through the barrier to cross the road and retrace your way back to Majors Car Park.

Common Lizard

Walk 18
The Magnificent Severn
Wolverley

Today it's difficult to imagine this great river, now a prime weekend retreat from the industrial conurbation, as it used to be. Over the centuries it has been a power source, a transport network, and a home for both industry and commerce. During this century rapid technological advances have resulted in this timeless river being restored to one of peace and beauty. This outstanding walk starts from Wolverley – a Worcestershire village perched around a sandstone outcrop – though any convenient point on the circuit would do as well.

Since I first walked this circuit some years ago, about 9 miles of it has become part of the Worcestershire Way (WW) – a long distance regional footpath running 36 miles from Kinver to Malvern. Consequently the route from Solcum Farm to Bewdley is very well waymarked

---

DISTANCE: 17 miles
MAPS: Landranger (1:50,000) 138. Pathfinder (1:25,000) 932,933,952 and 953
PARKING: Wolverley (limited), Eymore Wood Car Park, Arley Car Parks and Bewdley Car Parks.
PUBLIC TRANSPORT: Midland Red West Service 5/5A from Kidderminster. Alight at Wolverley Sebright First School. Walk forward to pass the church and arrive at the village centre.
Alternatively Midland Red West Service 192/292 Birmingham - Hereford. Alight at Bewdley, then take up the walk from ➤ on page 100.
START/FINISH: Wolverley (GR 829793)

FROM the centre of Wolverley village leave the Queens Head pub and walk uphill to pass the Court House which dates from 1620. Just before the traffic lights, and opposite Gloster House, take the signed and waymarked footpath on the left and follow it to reach a stile into a field. Walk a short way forward to a second stile which you cross to then turn immediately right to the top of a slope where another stile takes you onto Drakelow Lane.

Go left along Drakelow Lane where, in a little over a quarter of a mile and on the right, you will see a footpath sign for Blakeshall Lane. Turn right to follow the drive to Solcum House – which also doubles as the

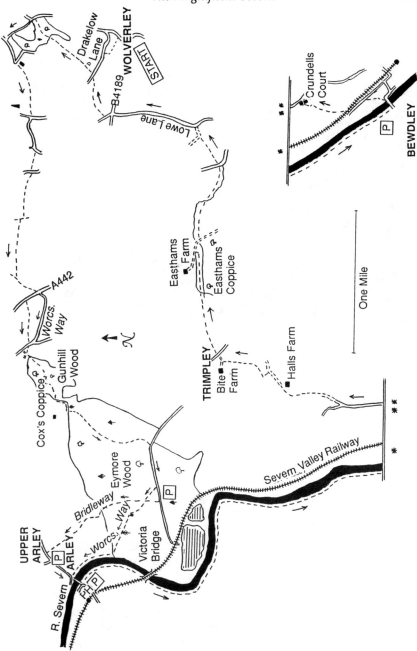

WOLVERLEY

Drakelow Lane

START

B4189

Lowe Lane

Crundells Court

BEWDLEY

P

A442

Worcs. Way

Easthams Farm

Easthams Coppice

One Mile

Gunhill Wood

TRIMPLEY

Bite Farm

Halls Farm

N

Cox's Coppice

Severn Valley Railway

Eymore Wood

UPPER ARLEY

P

Bridleway

Worcs. Way

ARLEY

P

Victoria Bridge

P P

R. Severn

Wolverley Court House

footpath – and arriving at the gable end of the house continue forward with the tarmac drive to a point immediately in front of the ornamental gates on the left. On your right there is a step stile in the fence that you cross to then go left and follow the fence on your original line. At a gate and fence stile continue forward to a stile leading into a large field.

In this field there is a tendency for walkers to go straight ahead across the field and thereby enter the opposite woodland at the incorrect point. Your objective is in fact the far right inverted corner of the woodland at its lowest point. To achieve this the right of way heads for the corner, ever so slightly right and on a bearing of 40 degrees, through the lowest part of the field. At the corner you will see an obvious gap into the trees and in a few yards a fence on the left.

Now follow the distinct path and the fence up through the plantation to a stile. Continue up to another stile at the side of a house and so onto Blakeshall Lane.

Turn left to follow the lane and then left again at a T-junction. Arriving at another T-junction ignore the public footpath sign opposite and instead go left along the lane signed 'No Through Road – Dead End – Except Footpath'. Pass Moat Court Farm and Solcum Stables to reach a sharp left bend at the white 'Solcum Farm'. Here go straight ahead along the grassy right hand edge of the house to a gate with a stile at its right and a public footpath sign for 'Kingsford Lane ¼ mile'. Cross the stile and walk down a valley where in a while you will see compounded buildings on the right that are the visible parts of World War II underground factories. A little further on you will also see good examples of rock dwellings. Soon the valley path broadens to tarmac and goes through a plant hire yard and then a gate to reach Kingsford Lane.

Opposite is Sladd Lane and a telephone kiosk. Cross over and follow Sladd Lane for about a third of a mile as far as a left bend where there is a static caravan site opposite. Go through the site gate – signed 'Public Footpath Bodenham Lane' – to follow the concrete road forward and up to the very top of the site where there is a metal wicket gate onto a very narrow lane. Turn left for 30 yards and then go over the signed stile on the right and forward with a fence on the left to soon cross another stile. In the next field go half right in the direction of the arrow and walk up a small slope to meet the left fence and, under an oak tree, a waymarked stile. On the other side continue forward and up, now with a hedge on your right, to the topmost corner of the field where there is another stile – partly camouflaged by a tree – onto a crossing track.

On the cross track go right for 25 yards to a gateway and stile into a field. Go through and turn instantly left with the fence and walk up the steep slope to a stile in the top left corner of the field. Pause here to regain your breath and look back at the rolling landscape that stretches all the way to the Clent Hills. Continuing, cross the stile and again walk upwards with a hedge and fence on your left to a stile just before the brow. On the other side go forward with a fence on your right to follow it over the brow. At the top the views right are quite something. Just beyond the brow you will quickly reach a gate and step stile onto a vehicle track. Turn left and follow the track as it skirts the Wildlife Sanctuary and Fishery to then meet the A442.

Here you have a choice, both of which re-join in a short distance.

Directly across the A442 is a tarmac road which is the Worcestershire Way and which you can follow for half a mile to a T-junction with another road. Then continue from ➡ *(p. 98).*

However, if you support those who believe that our rights of way should be walked at every opportunity; if you don't mind the possibility of some overgrowth or crops; and if you dislike road walking; then this alternative is for you.

At the A442 turn right and follow the pavement for 130 yards to the first 'Wildlife Sanctuary and Fishery' sign. On the opposite side of the road (left) is a large oak tree and near it a gate and public footpath sign. Cross over and pass through the gate to walk the edge of the long field with the fence on your right. In the top corner cross a stile next to a yellow Portacabin and follow the hedged and fenced path to another stile to then pass between 'Rosemary Cottage' and 'Bank Cottage' and so onto a road. Just a few yards to your left is the T-junction of the WW alternative with its two wooden signs.

➥ Whichever alternative you have chosen do follow the sign indicating the 'Viewpoint 80m' which is well worth the slight detour.

Having visited the viewpoint retrace you steps and pass 'Rosemary Cottage' and 'Bank Cottage' on the right just beyond which there is a bridleway sign on the left at the edge of a grassed area with trees. Leave the road and follow the direction of the sign across the green and pass right of a large, spreading oak tree with a 'Glovewood' sign attached to it. In a few yards you will meet a footpath sign on the side of a track that points into the drive for 'Woodcot'. Follow the sign and pass left of the chalet type bungalow to continue on a broad track into Cox's Coppice. Arriving at another chalet bungalow – 'Wood House' – pass left of it to a waymarked gate.

Through the gate go forward on a broad, grassy track down and through Gunhill Wood – you are now starting the long descent into the Severn Valley – and after a while arrive at a stile on the edge of the woodland and a pasture. In the pasture go left with the edge and then right to the lowest bottom corner where steps take you down to cross a footbridge.

You are now entering Eymore Wood, home to lots of pheasants, lots of grey squirrels and a few deer. Still on the Worcestershire Way – it now follows a public footpath through Eymore Wood for three quarters of a mile – a profusion of tracks, forestry roads and fire breaks gives it the appearance of a twisting but well waymarked route.

Leaving the footbridge follow the path up to join, and go left with, a green cross track. Continuing with it soon brings you to a broad grassy cross track where you swing right and in a few yards arrive at another grassy track where you go right again to follow this broad ride down through the trees for some distance. On a bend you merge with a broad forestry road and then continue forward in the same direction for some way before crossing a bridge and then reaching FRP 6. Here the forestry road swings right but you continue straight ahead with the WW sign on a broad grassy track. As it soon begins to descend look for the way-marked path on the left that leaves the track to enter the trees. Following the path reach a 'green cross road' where you turn right to descend to a culverted stream. Over the stream the track swings right but you leave

Loco. 75069 crossing the Severn by the Victoria Bridge
(Severn Valley Railway)

Photo: Pat Arrowsmith

it on the bend to take the waymarked steps up to a fence and stile. Cross the stile onto a road where you turn right.

Follow the road for 300 yards where, on the right, there is a gate, a footpath sign and a WW marker – Eymoor Wood car park is a little further along the road. Go through the gate to re-enter the woodland and follow the track down soon meeting a crossroad of tracks. Here again you have a choice.

The crossing track is in fact a public bridleway and if you wish you can turn right to follow it through the woodland – it is periodically signed by the simple expedient of a horseshoe on a wooden post. Leaving the wood the bridleway becomes a hedged/fenced green lane that can be followed to the tarmac road just above Arley. A left turn along the road will bring you into Arley village at the footbridge across the River Severn. Then continue from ▪▪▪➧ (p. 100)

Perhaps the more scenic route is to follow the Worcestershire Way and to do this you simply go straight ahead at the track crossroads. Descend with the way and ignoring the right turn to Huntsfield Farm cross a culverted stream and follow the woodland edge. As your track rises it then swings left back into the woodland, you however continue forward directly to metal gates with a private sign. To your right you will see a stile that you cross to go left with the fenced path to a hunter's gate behind a cottage. Through the gate you enter a sloping field where ahead, and slightly left, you will see a marker pole that leads you down through a hedge gap and ferns to a stile taking you back into the woodland.

Over the stile follow the clear path down and forward through attractive mixed woodland. In a while your path descends to a wooden signpost where steps go down to a cross track. Go straight across and descend to cross a footbridge to the side of the River Severn. Now follow the clear elevated path all the way upstream to meet houses and then the footbridge in Arley.

➠ There are amenities in Arley so do have a browse around before using the metal footbridge to reach the west bank of the river.

On the other side of the river you have a further choice. Assuming that the Severn Valley Railway is running, you can take a steam train to Bewdley and rejoin the walk there. Alternatively you can follow the WW signs downstream to Bewdley and enjoy four miles of superb riverside walking.

Following the second option you will pass under Victoria Bridge which carries the Severn Valley Railway across the river. Cast and erected in 1861 by the famous Coalbrookdale Company it is a favourite spot for steam train photographers. To see a locomotive in full steam crossing the river is indeed an impressive sight. Further along the river you will also pass under the pipeline bridge carrying Birmingham's water supply from mid-Wales and, just before Bewdley, you will then see solitary stone pillars standing in the river bed. These are all that remain of the bridge that carried a line from the Wyre Forest to join the Severn Valley Railway. This riverside walk goes some way to explain how the old G.W.R. earned the nickname 'God's Wonderful Railway'.

Bewdley itself is a handsome town. Once a river port it has many buildings associated with its historic trading importance and as such is worthy of exploration – but allow plenty of time!

➤ *Alternative starting point using public transport.*

Cross Telford's road bridge in Bewdley to the east bank of the river and on the right bend go left to pass the entrances of 'Woodeave' and 'Glenhurst' in quick succession and almost as quickly, arrive at the gates to Bewdley Bowling Club. To the right of the gates is a hedged and fenced footpath that you follow as it passes the bowling green and quickly brings you to trees on the edge of a static caravan site. A minor path goes right to follow the edge of the site but yours is more distinct and goes forward and across a service road to cross the grassy centre of the site. Leave the caravan site through the main gate to join a narrow road and then turn left.

Follow the road, passing Riverway Drive, until reaching a public footpath sign on the right that directs you through a bridge under the Severn Valley Railway. Immediately cross a stile into a sloping field and walk forward and up the lowest part of a little valley with trees left and scrub right. At the crescent shaped top follow a fairly clear path slightly right of an oak tree to a gateway in the top right corner of the field. Pass through and now follow the hedged and fenced track to a gate and stile. Go forward, now with just the hedge on your left, to reach the top left corner of this field. In the corner and left there is a gate and step stile that you cross into another field.

In this field go half right to cut the immediate field corner and arrive at the protruding corner of wooden ranch fencing – a bearing of 340 degrees. On the other side of the fence is a duck pond. Walk forward with the fence on your right and soon arrive in a corner where there is a stile and footpath sign. Cross over onto the service drive to the barn conversions – Crundalls Court – and go forward to cross a cattle grid onto a tarmac lane.

Turn left along the lane and follow it as it rises gently for almost half a mile to the entrance of 'The Riddings' on the left. Here the lane's status becomes more that of a hedged track which bears right – a waymark arrow confirming it – to then pass the entrances to 'Yewlands' and 'Martindale'. Continuing with your hedged track meet a gate into a large field and prepare yourself for some terrific views.

Walk up the field edge, with the hedge on your right, heading towards Hall's Farm. Before the top you pass a gate into a field on the right and continue forward for just over 100 yards to another gate before the field corner. Before going through the gate, which has a partly overgrown stile at the side, pause to admire the views left across the Severn Valley and the Wyre Forest to the Clee Hills. Once through the gate go forward for 40 yards to a point where on your left there is a gate with a sign 'Private Property – Keep Out'. Here you join a track coming from that gate to then go right with it to a gate left of the farmhouse. Pass through the gate and walk between a metal barn left and a brick barn right and then go right and left with the track to now pass between an orchard left and a silo tower right. Your track now merges with another coming in from the right to form what is now an unsurfaced lane. Continue forward to pass a pylon in the hedge where the lane now becomes surfaced and in another 50 yards arrive at a slight bend where, on the left and next to the entrance to 'Hillcrest', there is a gate and stile.

Cross the stile into a wide hedged track and follow it for the 40 yards it takes to reach a gate into a field. Through the gate turn right to follow garden fences to a stile in the field corner. In the next field go half left to a stile in the fence ahead. This is left of a prominent oak tree and on a line for the end of the house left of the tree – a bearing of 10 degrees. Over the stile continue on the same line to cross another stile and then pass between the oak tree and the house to a gate leading onto the tarmac drive of Bite Farm. On the drive go right – while admiring a substantial herd of pygmy goats – and follow it to a road.

At the road go straight over where there is an unusually wide roadside verge. Follow the path through the 50 yards of verge scrub to meet a fence stile in a field corner near a telegraph pole. Go over the stile into the field and walk forward with a garden hedge on your right to a gate and step stile in the corner.

In the next field walk ahead between two oak trees in the middle – a bearing of 75 degrees – and in the field boundary opposite you will see a short section of wooden fence left of a concrete water trough. Cross the fence stile here into a sloping field where on the same line and just below the crest you will see the tops of three trees. Walk to them – they are in a hedge – and make for the right hand one. Here swing right for 25 yards to the end of the hedge and to a gate in a fence. Go through into a steeply sloping field and, initially following the left hand wire fence down, bear gently right to the far right corner in the lowest part of the pasture. In the corner is a stile giving access into Easthams Coppice.

Now follows a mile of what must compare with some of the finest walking in the country.

Entering Easthams Coppice go forward through the pretty shallow valley with the aptly named Honey Brook on your right. Soon arriving at a stile in a fence go over onto the farm track to turn right and shortly pass old sheds and farm machinery on the left. Behind them is a sandstone escarpment with old rock dwellings. Follow the track a little further where it becomes sandy and you arrive at a slight right hand bend and a metal gate on the left. Go through the gate, or over the fence stile at the side, to enter a beautifully green valley.

Walk along the clear lush track to soon meet and follow the Honey Brook again. Shortly the track takes you over the stream to continue along the valley bottom now with the stream on your right. As you walk through the valley notice the ledge caves up on the left. Passing two footbridges on the right you will eventually arrive at a gate and stile before a white house. Go over and forward on the gravel drive for the few yards to the A442.

Across the main road is a footpath sign and a stile that you cross to go along a fenced path to a second stile at the top of the hill. Go over the stile into a field and continue forward to a gate in a hedge corner just left of a telegraph pole. At the left side of the gate you will notice an iron hurdle that you now cross to continue your line with the fence and hedge on your right to reach a gate and stile in the field corner. Cross the stile into a green lane at a bend. Go right (forward) to soon join the tarmac at Lowe Lane.

Follow the lane left for three quarters of a mile, passing a right junction and houses, to the cross roads with the B4189. Go straight across into Sladd Lane – signed for Kingsford Country Park – where on the right is a bench affording striking views across the valley. About 100 yards into Sladd Lane is a public bridleway on the right, signed for Drakelow Lane. Go with it along the drive to Hillhouse Cottage to pass through a gate and arrive at a second gate immediately in front of the house. To your left is a white metal fence and a garage wall and you will see that the bridleway goes between them. Take the well trodden way and in a few yards it swings right with the white fence to go steeply down a wooded slope to a valley bottom and a footbridge.

Cross the footbridge and follow the fenced way up the other side to meet Drakelow Lane. Turn right along the lane and, just for a slight variation, follow it all the way to a T-junction at the single file traffic lights. Here turn right and follow the narrow road into the centre of Wolverley.

Continue reading from the beginning if you started from Bewdley.

Canada Goose

Index

Also from Meridian...

THE NAVIGATION WAY
A hundred mile towpath walk, by Peter Groves and Trevor Antill

Starting from the centre of Birmingham and encompassing fourteen West Midlands canals the Navigation Way follows a meandering course through varied urban areas, rich in historical associations, and through delightful countryside, until terminating at Chasewater reservoir. It is described in twelve sections to provide a series of walks ranging from 5¼ to 11 miles.

This fully revised and extended second edition also contains ten additional circular 'canal-link' walks, from 3½ to 9 miles in length, which will enable you to savour some of the attractive walking areas adjacent to the canals.
1993 ISBN 1-869922-19-0. £4.95. 112 pages. 31 b/w photographs. 24 maps. Paperback. A5.

RIDGES and VALLEYS
Walks in the Midlands, by Trevor Antill

A selection of walks within the counties of Shropshire, Staffordshire and the old county of Worcestershire taking in some of the better known, and some lesser known hills; and most with one or two pleasant surprises. Distances range from three to ten miles, with a 'Challenge Walk' of twenty miles which can, however, easily be split into smaller sections. Full parking and public transport details are provided.
ISBN 1 869922 15 8. £3.95. 96 pages. 12 photographs. 19 maps.

HIDDEN HEREFORDSHIRE
A Book of Country Walks, by Julie Meech

A churchyard awash with spring daffodils, a river bordered with ancient willows, a unique Norman church with comic, grotesque and erotic carvings, a fourteenth century dovecote with 666 nesting places, a Neolithic burial chamber, countless medieval timber-framed buildings, a chance to see the rare Red Kite — these are but a few of the delights encountered in this book of twenty circular walks. Distances range from five to ten and a half miles, with a longer Black Hill walk of sixteen miles. With sketch maps, car parking instructions, details of public transport, notes of the walking conditions, and the location of pubs, food shops and tea-rooms.
ISBN 1-869922-16-6. £4.95. 112 pages. 21 photographs. 20 maps.

WATERSIDE WALKS in the MIDLANDS
by Birmingham Ramblers, edited by Peter Groves

Ranging in distance from three to twelve miles the twenty-two walks in this book feature brooks, streams, pools, rivers and canals, in their many aspects. Some can be found a short distance from the centre of Britain's second city; others will take the reader further afield in the West Midlands and into the attractive counties of Warwickshire, Worcestershire, Shropshire, Staffordshire and Derbyshire. With car parking and public transport details.
ISBN 1 869922 09 3. £3.95. 112 pages. 28 photographs. 22 maps.

Prices may be subject to revision.
From all booksellers or, in case of difficulty, direct from the publishers. Please send your order to: **Meridian Books, 40 Hadzor Road, Oldbury, Warley, West Midlands B68 9LA.** Orders should be accompanied by the appropriate remittance, adding the following amounts for postage and packing: Orders value up to £5.00 add 75p; over £5.00 add £1.00.
Please send s.a.e. for our full catalogue of books on walking, local and county guides, and local history.